TWELVE RECIPES

WILLIAM MORRO
An Imprint of HarperCollinsPubli

Twelve Recipes

Cal Peternell

HarperCollins books may be purchased for educational, business, or sales promotional use. For information please e-mail the Special Markets Department at SPsales@harpercollins.com.

FIRST EDITION

Designed by Lorie Pagnozzi

Photographs by Ed Anderson/Styling by George Dolese

Illustrations by Liam Peternell, Milo Henderson, Henderson Peternell, and Kathleen Henderson

Library of Congress Cataloging-in-Publication Data has been applied for.

ISBN 978-0-06-227030-6

14 15 16 17 18 ID6/QG 10 9 8 7 6 5 4 3 2 1

To Mom and Dad, who showed me, night after night, the subtle, profound, and lasting value of gathering around the table for a family meal

CONTENTS

Twelve Recipes

FOREWORD

michael pollan

The simple act of cooking a meal has become so thickly crusted with pretension and anxiety that it's no wonder so few Americans feel comfortable in the kitchen anymore. But who would have thought that exactly the antidote we need—this book—would come out of one of the most storied restaurant kitchens in America?

Actually, it's not completely surprising. Alice Waters has made a habit of hiring cooks who are not professional chefs but rather various kinds of quasi-normal people who just happen to have a passion for cooking. Artists, for example, which is what Cal Peternell was before he was hired to cook at Chez on the strength of the little zucchini frittatas he pan-fried for his tryout lunch. The place might be a temple of gastronomy, but it's always been infused with the spirit of the amateur.

Anyway, this is the book I have been waiting for, the one I'll be giving to all those friends who tell me they can't cook. *Twelve Recipes* is a resolutely informal, handwritten invitation to come back into the kitchen and learn the basics from a dude so chill that you will quickly forget he's also a brilliant cook. *It's just not that big a deal,* Cal quickly has you thinking, whether you're braising a quick sugo for pasta or making a pot of beans or simply boiling some vegetables because they're so fresh you just need to get out of their way. Have you ever called your mother or father to have them walk you step-by-step through a cherished-but-not-yet-mastered family recipe? This book reads a lot like that phone call in its ideal form—conversational, patient, calming, and lucid.

In fact, it was a flurry of such phone calls, long-distance from Cal's oldest son off at college, that inspired this book. Cal realized he had neglected to equip his son with one of the critical life skills everyone must have in order to live a healthy and happy life: how to cook a basic repertoire of dishes and a handful of sauces. Hence *Twelve Recipes*, "a meal manual for my sons leaving home, and all sons and daughters, to learn to cook and eat simply and well, with pleasure and good health."

Yet if the book is intended as a handbook for beginners, it has much to offer the more experienced cook, too. If anything, *Twelve Recipes* under-promises and overdelivers: beyond the big twelve, Cal proposes a great many delicious variations on the basic themes, plus a handful of clutch sauces that will improve anything they touch, whether a plate of pasta, a grilled piece of fish, or a boiled naked vegetable. If the recipes in this book constituted your entire repertoire, you would not be in bad shape at all.

But that's probably not how it will go. Because one of the best things about this deceptively simple, gracefully written book is just how competent and adventurous it will make you feel, not to mention hungry. I'm betting you will finish *Twelve Recipes* inspired to try all kinds of new dishes and to crack your neglected old cookbooks, bringing to them a whole new chill attitude: *It's just not that big a deal.*

alice waters

It is a rare and beautiful thing to pick up a book, thumb through the opening pages, and know without a doubt that you will love it from beginning to end. *Twelve Recipes* is one of those books. From the first few sentences, I was smiling—not only because of Cal's distinctive voice and wonderfully dry sense of humor, but because I knew I was in the best of hands.

Cal tells us that the germ of this book began when his oldest son, Henderson, moved away for college, and would call home for cooking guidance. I remember when my own daughter, Fanny, went away for school. I sent her off with recipes for all her favorite meals, but in those first few months I fielded the very same phone calls that Cal describes getting from his son. "How," Fanny would ask me, "am I supposed to roast a chicken?" The funny thing was, I suspected she already *knew* how to roast a chicken—but she wanted to hear me tell it again. There is something both sweet and important about the passing of recipes from mother to daughter, or from father to son. It is not just technique, but the comfort of home that you are passing along in those dishes and recipes, a comfort that kids are so in need of when they light out on their own for the first time and start learning to live as adults.

The foundation of *Twelve Recipes* is built on those sorts of universal foods that would-be cooks (young and old) know and love: toast, eggs, pasta, vegetables, and, yes, roast chicken. Learn your way around one simple recipe from each category, Cal reasons, and you are well on your way to knowing how to cook. Each of these foods comes alive through Cal's vivid writing and stories of his family's gustatory adventures, and with a casual, light touch he shows how to take these ingredients and make them shine. Take marinara sauce, for example: "We often do make a plain and satisfying sauce from just onions, a little garlic, and a can of tomatoes. I will give you that recipe and it's very good indeed, and great with meatballs but . . . if it is summer, and maybe you grew some tomatoes, or a friend did, or you found some irresistible and ripe at the market, there is also a fresh marinara that can be profoundly good, like the summer sun itself came down, put on an apron, and made you lunch. Okay, I'll give you that recipe, too." (I have had it, a basil and garlic-inflected five-minute affair with swirls of fresh ricotta, and can attest to its sublimity.)

I have always admired the simplicity, clarity, and deliciousness of the food Cal creates—he has brought tremendous talent and creativity to the kitchen at Chez Panisse over the years. He has a background in painting, and his extraordinary artistry extends to the beautiful way he assembles a plate. But perhaps just as extraordinary is the way young cooks learn from Cal. He is one of the greatest teachers I know, and it is because he knows how to empower the cooks—not dictating to them but encouraging them, allowing them to go at their own pace, quietly instilling in them the important principles of aliveness and beauty in food.

Twelve Recipes perfectly captures Cal's subtle, relaxed teaching style. He applies his artist's sense of flavor and proportion to create a practical road map for cooking at home—the sort of robust, soul-satisfying meals you want to make for your family and friends, the kind of cooking that brings everyone to the table. For Cal, cooking is an appealingly malleable thing. He shows that to be a cook involves not only making mistakes sometimes, but having fun making them—and that openness leads to surprising discoveries. "One night, mid–ragù finto making, I suddenly turned Thai-ward," he writes, "inspired, for some reason, to leave the pasta for another time." (The happy result of this detour is a Thai larb of ground pork.) This is one of his most crucial lessons: a meal doesn't need to be a fixed and anchored affair. You can change course halfway through, break some rules while sticking by a few others, make the best of whatever you have on hand, and let your instincts and your senses guide you to what is delicious. What better way to bring our children into the kitchen?

Cal is not the only artist in the Peternell family—as you read through this book, you might see, among other things, a cheese grater drawn by his wife, Kathleen, a tiny roast chicken penned by Henderson, a bag of beans by Milo, a vegetable sketch by young Liam. The whole book is a labor of love, a celebration of family and home and deliciousness. *Twelve Recipes* is an edible education in the truest sense: learning how to approach the kitchen with confidence, humor, and a sense of adventure is the surest way to foster a love of food and cooking. That is one of the greatest gifts we can give our children—and ourselves.

INTRODUCTION

Ten years into my nearly twenty-year tenure at Chez Panisse, a rare quirk in kitchen staffing left us with too many chefs in the kitchen. In an attempt to save the broth from being spoiled, I offered myself up as a dreamy solution: I would take one for the team, helpfully decamping for a three-month sabbatical in Europe with my wife and our three sons. I only half believed it could happen and was as shocked as anyone when my request was approved and the pieces began to fall into place.

We had limitless enthusiasm for travel but somewhat limited funds. Luckily, we had friends to stay with along the way and found surprisingly cheap tickets to Dublin, as good a place as any to begin our travels . . . except that Ireland was in the midst of an economic boom and turned out to be breathtakingly expensive. We spent too much and made the amateur mistake of driving too many hours to too many destinations, all with three boys crammed in the backseat of our wee rental car. We were stressed by the end of the week and hungry—other than pints, crisps, and one wonderful meal in Shanagarry, we'd found nothing much good to eat—and eagerly boarded our Dangerously Cheap Airlines flight to Paris, where old friends had given us their flat for ten days while they were out of town. We immediately put a comfortable routine into place that started with three chocolate croissants and two cafés au lait every morning. We'd brush the crumbs off the kids, wipe the foamy milk off our upper lips, and then wander Paris all day, bumping and portaging one-year-old Liam's stroller over cobblestones and many sets of métro stairs. A museum, lunch, a park or an ice cream in the afternoon, and we'd make a stop to buy groceries for dinner on the way home: a spacious loft preloaded with plenty of toys and books to keep Liam happy, and with a kitchen ready for real cooking. The older boys, thirteen-year-old Henderson and ten-year-old Milo, did the homework their school had sent along for the trip while I cooked dinner and opened a bottle of wine. An American chef in Paris, and we did not eat a single dinner out in ten days. Everything that is charming about a nice dinner in a restaurant—the relaxed pace, carefully set table, red wine, and white tablecloths—can turn frustrating and absurd when your kids are tired, hungry, and starting to squirm.

This pleasant, practical lunch-out/dinner-in rhythm continued contentedly through the rest of our travels. Naturally, there were memorable bites out along the way—Milo nibbling the comb from the head atop a sausage-stuffed chicken neck that looked like an in-the-flesh version of a Pez dispenser; Liam toddling to what seemed like every puddle in Venice, and either falling in or carefully dipping his finger between the cobblestones and taking a wet taste before we could stop him; Henderson settling, once the chocolate croissants were out of range, on a steady diet of the cheese ravioli in ragù and orange Fanta served at every trattoria—but the best meals were the ones we cooked and ate in our guest-home kitchens.

Returning stateside, I began puzzling over why more cooking isn't done at home, even, or maybe especially, among my friends who are professional chefs. Too tired, too hungry, wanting to see what's happening at the other restaurants—these are legitimate reasons to go out and get a taco, a slice, or a fancy meal, but for me, staying home and cooking with family and friends is the best relaxation. I am not entirely alone in this: there are plenty of us: chefs for whom cooking at home is instinctual, habitual. Sure, we love the drama and performance involved in preparing and serving meals at our restaurants, but we love at least as well the depth and intimacy of cooking at home for our families and friends. The ancient acts of gathering foods, cooking them, and then coming together to eat are as profound as any that we do, and as pleasurable. My career in restaurants has been a happy success, landing me in charge of the beautiful kitchens at Chez Panisse in Berkeley. Still, I consider cooking and eating with my family my best skill, and so it was with a little surprise, and a little shame, that I realized my eldest son was only a summer away from leaving home for college, and I hadn't taught him, or the other kids, how to cook. Well, I sort of had. I mean, we cook together some and eat together more. They have always watched me cook, drawn as boys are to the sharp knives and speedy strokes that their attention encouraged, even in a grown-up boy like me. They baked cookies from the recipe on the bag of chocolate chips like every other kid and experimented with flavorings for their glasses of milk, mixing concoctions as if they were Harry Potter's potions. Back on earth, I would assign a little garlic pounding, herb picking, and cream whipping to get them into the kitchen, and they certainly were masters of the coming-together-to-eat part, but the actual gathering-and-cooking-of-the-food part . . . well, I guess I thought that would just be effortlessly communicated and instinctively absorbed. And probably some did sink in, but now that the first of the boys was moving away and would have to feed himself out there in the world, I wondered if I had been explicit enough, had neglected to codify some of the basics. Surely he knew how salty the water must taste before the pasta went in, but had I warned strongly enough against the danger of burning the garlic for the sauce? We'd roasted plenty of chickens together, but what about braises—had we covered those at all? So useful! Grocery shopping had always been an avoid-if-possible bore for the boys and a welcome escape for me, but now I worried that though Henderson had heard me preach about the importance of excellent ingredients and that cooking starts at the market, I hadn't taken him, basket in hand, and shown him how to do it! Emergency tutorial was needed, and with just a summer to go, we'd have to hurry.

A crash course in cooking for yourself and others also goes by another name: it's called dinner. Sometimes it's a party and sometimes just a meal, but cooking lessons tend to end with everyone eating. We crammed and ate that summer, trying to fit in the essentials between our jobs and Ping-Pong rallies, with my student text messaging a faraway girlfriend and sleeping *very* late, even, some days, into the dinner-prep hours. I swallowed the lecture on the importance of promptness and instead stressed the usefulness of a timer when boiling eggs, making crostini, or toasting nuts in the oven, hoping he might make the connection. Meals—many of them—were eventually made and consumed, good food made great by the intimacy of the table.

We got through much of my repertoire, but the phone calls began within a week of his departure to the East Coast: cooking queries that both charmed (he was actually cooking!) and alarmed (I *knew* we hadn't got to all of it—and what if I hadn't been able to pick up the phone!). And as good as I have gotten at narrative recipes over the phone—we get a lot of calls for help at the restaurant—I soon realized that what we were experiencing was the germ of a cookbook. Once you've cooked something a dozen times, a written recipe becomes unnecessary. Until then, it is good to have a reference, a cookbook for not just getting by but for really feeding yourself: a meal manual for my sons leaving home, and all sons and daughters, to learn to cook and eat simply and well, with pleasure and good health.

This is a manuscript sent from father to sons to codify a core group of recipes. It's the book my sons will turn to when they can't reach me by phone, and the book everyone else can turn to because they don't have my number. This is neither a lifestyle guide nor an ethical screed but a set of directions for succeeding with simple, delicious dishes, for bouncing back when you fail, and to turn to when you're ready for the next level.

Young Liam, perhaps sick of watching me work on this book, suggested that the title should be *Infinity Recipes.* It's true, there are many more than twelve, and factoring in variations, let's face it, we *are* approaching infinity. But from the start, I felt that if you could pare it down and learn just twelve recipes, one from each of the chapters, say, that you'd be pretty set. Another dozen would broaden your options, and with each added dozen, your perception of cooking itself would broaden to include the satisfaction of making, the pleasure of eating, and the opportunity to share that satisfaction, pleasure, and love in the kitchen and around the table.

how to cook with this book

For each recipe, I have included a basic version and variations. I've chosen the basic version based on simplicity and at-home popularity. I don't deny that this ranking is often arbitrary, and if you find that the variation becomes the basic version in your kitchen, I celebrate your decision and excellent taste.

I recommend that you read through the entire book before beginning to cook. Just kidding (sort of), but I do suggest reading the whole recipe before you start to cook it: the order in which things are done is often of great importance and there are detailed instructions for certain techniques that you may find useful. Also, you might want to go straight to one of the variations listed after the basic recipe.

In an effort to avoid anything like intimidation, I try not to demand too much in terms of specific ingredients and equipment and encourage substitutions, to a point. Take mirepoix, aka soffritto, the aromatic combination of onions, carrots, and celery, chopped more or less finely, that is the base of so many dishes: there are good reasons that each would be missed from the mix, but that doesn't mean you shouldn't go ahead without any one of them. But it does mean that when you are short a vegetable or two and have to do without, you should take notice of where the deep savory satisfaction of the onion, the color and earthy sweetness of the carrot, and the herbal fragrance of the celery are missing.

breakable rules

There are a few things you should know before you begin cooking. These are not rules so much as starting places and are often also embedded in specific recipes.

- This first rule is actually not breakable: taste everything and taste often. This is the most important thing you can do to succeed in making delicious food. Taste the ingredients as you cook: when they are raw, cooking, and cooked. The best cooks respond to what they discover through constant tasting. When you know it needs something but you just can't tell what, spoon a little aside into a bowl and experiment a bit. More salt, lemon, vinegar, oil . . . stir in a little and see if you were right. When you've got it, adjust the whole batch.

- It is an enduring truth that the best-tasting ingredients will yield the best-tasting dishes, but I believe as strongly that if you are missing things, or what you have is not the best, you should cook anyway. The ways in which various parts add up to the sum of a wonderful meal are many. The quality of the ingredients and the way they are prepared are important, sure, but so are the personalities of the group of eaters . . . their moods . . . the room . . . the occasion. The right equation will make the table a success, even if the salad wilts, the meat is overcooked, or the cake falls.

• Get your timing right: while it's okay, for example, for the sauce to be done before the pasta, the other way around doesn't work. Figuring out which things can hold well and which need to be served right away is an essential skill. I like using a timer for certain things (especially when they're in the oven and out of sight)—not because when it goes off, I know whatever I'm cooking is done, but because I'll know that I need to check it, poke it, taste it to see if it is. It takes a while to get the hang of timing a meal right; just keep trying and pay attention to your mistakes.

• Go, right now, and soak some dried beans in a lot of cold water. I'll wait here. Tomorrow, when you're cooking them, you'll thank me.

• Whenever you just can't decide what to cook, buy a pork shoulder or at least a big chunk of one. (Pork shoulder is commonly called butt. Why? Maybe because the actual butt of the pig is called the ham and there's got to be a butt, so the shoulder gets to be it. It's too good a word to go unused.) Season it generously with salt and pepper (toasted and ground fennel, coriander, and cumin, singly or in combination, are nice too), wrap it back up, and put it in the fridge overnight. Tomorrow, when you're cooking it and getting ready to eat it with

the beans, you'll thank me again . . . and again the next day and the next: pork shoulder lasts a long time and is useful in so many ways—in pastas, tacos, and sandwiches, alongside eggs, in soups . . .

• The term *leftovers* becomes less than accurate when you are cooking serially for yourself or a family. Sometimes it just makes good sense to make a lot—some foods, like soups, get better and better over a couple of days. Others take time to prepare, and maybe you're going to be really busy this week—these are not so much leftovers as they are already-cooked ingredients, and plans have been made for them to be a future meal, or part of one. Some cooked foods are fine, better even, if left at room temperature for a time. Others require quick chilling if you plan on keeping them around, and for those, the ideal is to go from hot to cold as quickly as possible. Covering will hold in the heat and slow the cooling process, so *never cover hot food* (except, I suppose, if your intention is to keep it hot, as in a thermos). Putting an uncovered container of hot soup or stew in the refrigerator is fine. The fridge has to work a little harder, but the soup will chill quickly and save better. If it's especially thick soup, give it a stir once in a while as it cools. When the soup is fully cold, *then* you can cover it.

• When I first started cooking in restaurant kitchens, a major challenge for me was the question of what size to cut vegetables for cooking. Terms were tossed around the kitchen—*brunoise, minced, diced, julienne.* They hadn't covered these in art school, so I sweated and bluffed my way through. At first, I lacked the knife skills. I got better, of course, but more important, I began to learn when it matters and when it doesn't. Mostly, it doesn't, and mistakes made at the cutting board can often be corrected at the stovetop. Chopped too big: cook it a little longer, a little hotter, maybe add a splash of water. Cut too small: well, is this ever really a problem? Teaching young cooks to use a knife in the kitchen can be harrowing, but the more they do, the better they get, and the fewer Band-Aids later on. I've seen it done brilliantly in a classroom full of eleven-year-olds with nary a nick and boorishly badly in many a commercial kitchen. Patience helps; intimidation doesn't.

• When cooking in a skillet, especially over high heat, the pan should be dry, without oil, until it's hot and ready for cooking. The oil should be added only then, and the food you are cooking should follow quickly and carefully. Oil left alone in a hot pan will soon burn and take on a noxious flavor that will affect the entire dish.

• I try to have two kinds of olive oil on hand, because while swirling the best extra-virgin oil onto a salad or garlicky grilled bread is a great idea, pouring it into a hot skillet is unnecessary. For that, use a lighter and more affordable olive oil, or do what I do and make a blend using 1 part fancy olive oil to 3 or 4 parts canola, grape seed, or other vegetable oil.

• Salty note: At home, we cook with sea salt—what a local mill, Giusto's, labels as extra fine. I like it for the texture, the way it feels in my fingers, and the flavor—a little less salty than my road salt, kosher. Table salt is too slippery and granular for cooking by hand.

• Cook with plenty of garlic, but know this:

* Before garlic goes into a pan, be sure you have something wet on hand (chopped tomatoes, greens, water, wine, stock, and so on) to add and keep it from burning.

* Once the garlic is in the pan, so must all your attention be. You cannot walk away or stop stirring, watching, smelling.

* When these recipes call for raw garlic, it is pounded. This means either I put a clove in a mortar with a pinch of salt and pound it until it is almost liquid, or I crush it on a cutting board with the side of a chef's knife, sprinkle salt on it, and chop it very fine, smearing it with the sides of the knife in between chopping until, as in the mortar, it is almost liquid. Decide for yourself how much, but a little raw garlic tends to go a long way.

* If you're peeling garlic and a sliver goes under your nail, it can really hurt. I use a paring knife to avoid the pain.

• Dried herbs are like dead flowers: if you can't bring them fresh, probably better to not bring them at all. Most dried herbs—parsley, basil, tarragon, and cilantro—are truly atrocious and can be ruinous, while others—thyme, rosemary, and sage—are grudgingly acceptable in certain applications. Dried oregano and bay leaves are the only ones that are really okay.

• Buy spices whole and in small amounts so that they stay fresh. The aromatic quality of spices is multiplied if they are toasted before grinding. Heat a small skillet to medium and add the seeds. When they start to hop around a little and smell spicy, shake the pan and toast for 15 seconds. Tip them into a mortar or spice mill and grind to powder, or leave them a little coarse for textural flavor bits.

• Nuts are best bought whole, in smallish amounts, and stored in the fridge so they don't go rancid. Toasting nuts before using improves their flavor and texture. Heat the oven to 350˚F. Spread the nuts on a baking sheet and roast them for 8 minutes (timer!). Cut one in half to check if it's done—it should be tan inside. If it's still pale, reset the timer for 3 minutes and put the nuts back in. When the nuts are toasted, set the baking sheet aside and let the nuts cool before using. Pine nuts are small enough that they can also be toasted in a skillet over low heat, shaken frequently.

• Though many restaurant cooks pack an impressive and bewildering array of knives, ask any of them and they'll tell you that if they had to choose one, it'd be the accurately named chef's knife. It's the one to use for chopping, slicing, and dicing—anything that you are cutting on a cutting board. They come in all sizes. I like an 8-inch chef's knife. A paring knife is very good to have, too, but not for use on a cutting board. Paring knives are best for, well, paring—when you are working in hand, like peeling an apple or a potato, or if you are cutting things like green beans into segments or strawberries into wedges. I admire other cooks' fancy paring knives but tend to buy cheaper ones myself, so I'm not as sad when I lose them. A little straight-bladed model is enormously handy, and one with a curved blade is called a bird's-beak—how can you not want that?

• Many recipes start with the cutting and proper cooking of that most useful ingredient, the onion. Here are some tips for using my desert island vegetable:

* *Sliced onions:* Using a chef's knife, cut only the littlest bit off both the root and stem ends of the onion. Cut in half from root to stem and peel each half with your fingers or a paring knife. Put the halves cut side down, and with a single, angled slice, cut a little wedge at the root end, removing the bit of the onion that's holding the layers together. Turn the half so that the root end is toward you, the stem away, and cut vertically, from pole to pole, making very thin, smile-shaped slices. Repeat with the other half.

* *Diced onions:* Using a chef's knife, cut only the littlest bit off both the root and stem ends of the onion. Cut in half from root to stem and peel each half with your fingers or a paring knife. Put the halves cut side down. From the stem end, make slices toward the root—your knife horizontal, parallel to the cutting board—but don't go all the way through. Now make slices vertically, from pole to pole, but again, not all the way through to the root end, which is holding it all together at this point, bless it. Now the glory: cut vertically across the other cuts, parallel with the onion's equator, and little dice will fall from your knife. With practice, no further chopping will be necessary, but if there are some chunky patches, go ahead and chop a bit.

* Cooking onions just right can be kind of tricky. It's important to cook them all the way, so they're not crunchy or raw tasting, but to not get them too brown, unless sweet caramelization is what you are aiming for. There's a temptation to use lots of oil, but that can get both greasy and expensive, so one way to sort of cheat is to add a little water to the pan. This is especially helpful if you're cooking with a thin-bottomed pan. Heavier sauté pans and cast-iron skillets make the job easier. So try adding a little water to give the onions a steamy head start, and then keep cooking over medium-low heat until they're soft and lightly browned.

• There are a number of other cooking techniques that are common to many different recipes. Learn them individually and then you can string them together in hundreds of ways, like dance moves or sign language. Explanations of these essential techniques are not included with every recipe in which they appear, but are often embedded in a representative recipe that can be referred back to. My ways of accomplishing certain tasks are certainly not the only ways, and may not always be the best for you, but over the years they have proven to work very well, so give them a try.

• These recipes are, with noted exceptions, for the amounts we ordinarily cook at home: enough for two adults and three hungry kids. Sometimes there are welcome leftovers; other times the platter is clear-cut.

EQUIPMENT RECOMMENDED

Wooden cutting board. Or two: I like to reserve one for fruit only so that it stays unscented by garlic or onions.

Large mortar and pestle (see page 80)

8-quart pasta pot

Big colander

Cheese planer (also handy for vegetables)

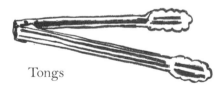

Tongs

Metal spatula

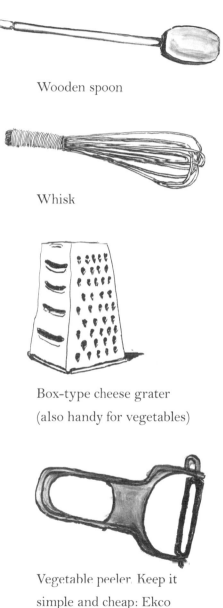

Wooden spoon

Whisk

Box-type cheese grater (also handy for vegetables)

Vegetable peeler. Keep it simple and cheap: Ekco swivel-bladed or Y-shaped peelers work well.

8-inch cast-iron pan. These are best bought used. Find them at yard sales, flea markets, and thrift shops, and look for a blackened pan with a smooth cooking surface, a dull shine, and no rust. Wagner Ware pans are deservedly classic.

Little bowl for salt

Pepper mill

8-inch chef's knife

Paring knife

Serrated bread knife

Can opener

Bamboo-handled spider. Useful for scooping things from boiling water or hot oil and also for pushing hard-boiled eggs or avocados through.

Wind-up timer (keep that phone in your pocket, mister)

Sieve

Mixing bowls, large, medium, and small

Salad spinner

Waiter's friend–style corkscrew

Ladle

MORE EQUIPMENT

9-inch cake pan. I like a deep 3-inch pan, but the more common 2-inch is fine as well.

Baking/casserole dish. A 3-quart, 13 x 9-inch Pyrex casserole is the one I use most. I also have a ceramic baking dish that is nice for bringing to the table.

12-inch sauté pan. I like All-Clad pans. Expensive but everlasting.

2- or 3-quart saucepan

Mouli food mill: the hand-cranked precursor to the blender. I see them often at yard sales and thrift shops.

Blender

Rubber spatula

Grill

Fire starter chimney

Wire brush for cleaning the grill grates

Potato masher

EQUIPMENT UNRECOMMENDED

Glass cutting board (scrape . . . cringe)

Salt and pepper shakers. These are knickknacks, which I like, but they are not tools.

Entire sets of serrated kitchen knives. Only one of your knives need be serrated.

Garlic press. It renders garlic too mashed for sautéing, too chunky to eat raw.

Nonstick-coated pans. Hmm . . . toxic budgie-killer at high heat? No thanks.

1

TOAST

There will not be a recipe here for taking a piece of sliced sandwich bread out of its wrapper and putting it in the toaster. That kind of toast is fine (if organic, or at least whole wheat, and hardly needs a recipe, though I do recommend buttering while hot) for when a hungry mouth needs filling or quieting. No, the toast of this chapter is a perfectly useful platform, a surprisingly flexible component, and an economical nosh. And if my dinner party crunch has become my dinner party crutch, well then, I lean on it proudly.

As with all cooking, the place to start making really good toast is at the market. Buy the best loaf of bread you can find—even if it's expensive—because you'll use every crumb. Get a big loaf, or maybe buy two so you can eat the fresh loaf with dinner and then save all uneaten bread in a bag—I keep leftover loaves, or parts of them, in plastic for a few days so they don't get hard as a rock and dangerous to slice. Bread stored this way for less than a week is usually pliant enough to be made into croutons or toasts, thick or thin, and a 1- to 3-day-old loaf can be revived back to table-ready status surprisingly well by rubbing it all over with wet hands, then popping it into a hot oven for 5 minutes or so. After that, if there's any left, I transfer it to a paper bag to fully dry without molding. Dry bread is ideal for smashing to crumbs and for thickening soups. If there's white or blue powdery mold on your stashed crusts, they're good only for the compost, the garbage, or the pigeons in the park.

Acceptable toast can be made from good bread in a pop-up toaster. Better, I find, is an oven—if it's already lit or you're making a lot of toasts—or a toaster oven. Because burned toast smells bad, I use a timer religiously when toasting bread. Nuts, too. It may seem amateur, but once the oven door is closed, I find it's all too easy to forget, so I set and reset. When a friend who was hanging out with me in the kitchen asked why I was, it seemed to her, obsessive with the dang-jangling timer, I said so that I didn't burn the croutons in the oven. She said the reason I forget is that I'm doing so many things at once: pounding garlic and anchovies, talking to her, washing greens, changing the record, opening wine, toasting. "Yes," I said, holding up my trusty wind-up timer, "and one little twist makes this whole beautiful world possible."

THIN CRISP TOAST

Thin crisp toast has never let me down. Making a batch while I mull over what's for dinner always saves me later when kids are circling or a guest arrives early. It's best made from stale bread—a fresh loaf is difficult to slice very thin, which is what you must do for crunchy, tender, non-mouth-injuring toast. A 350°F oven will crisp and lightly brown the bread with minimum risk of burning (timer!). Sprinkle olive oil onto a baking sheet, and then lay out the thinly sliced bread. Sprinkle or brush the slices with more oil and a little salt and shuffle, rubbing them together and soaking up whatever oil is on the pan. Rearrange the slices so they're all in a single layer again and toast for 7 minutes. Turn the pan front to back and toast for a few more minutes, if necessary, resetting the timer each time, until the toasts are golden brown all over with no pale patches. They will probably not all be done at the same time, so remove the ones that are, and keep toasting (timer!). Break off any parts that seem too dark. They do take some tending, but thin, crisp toasts will keep for a while—at least a couple of hours and for days if sealed in an airtight container.

Spread thin crisp toasts with **ricotta cheese** (or **cream cheese** or **cottage cheese** if you don't hate it), topped with a sprinkle of **olive oil**, salt, and black pepper . . . sliced **cold butter** and a little salt (I like a smear of **strong mustard** too, but I may be the only one) . . . sliced or smooshed-on **Hard-Boiled Eggs** (page 30) and **anchovies** . . . **hummus** (page 57) or other **bean paste** (page 52) . . . thin-sliced **tomatoes and basil** leaves . . . **smoked fish** or **thin slices of leftover grilled meats** and capery **Salsa Verde** (page 244) . . .

Crumbled thin crisp toasts also make great salad **croutons**.

THICK SOFT TOAST

Fresh bread is best for thick toast, though a 1- or 2-day-old loaf works fine, too. A 450°F oven will yield a slice with a golden, crunchy crust and a soft, hot interior. You can, of course, also use a toaster if you are just making a piece or two. Cut the bread ¾ inch thick. I prefer to oil or butter thick toast after toasting, so just place it on a baking sheet and toast it in the oven for 5 minutes. Or, if the rack in your oven seems clean, skip the baking sheet and put the slices right on the rack. When the timer that you remembered to set rings, and the toasts are nice and brown but still soft inside, they are done. Thick toast is for eating right away.

Without a doubt, the very best thing to do with thick toast is to rub the top with a raw garlic clove (the rough surface of the toast will grate the garlic in), be generous with your best olive oil, and sprinkle with a bit of salt. In season, rub half a tomato onto the toast after the garlic, crushing some of the flesh and juice into the bread before pouring on the oil. When these few ingredients are in top form, this may be the very best food, period.

Other things to put on thick toast: brown or white **beans** (Chapter 3) . . . **soup** of nearly any sort (Chapters 3 and 8) . . . an **egg**, poached (page 33), hard boiled (page 30), or softly scrambled (page 35) . . . **sautéed mushrooms** or **Sautéed Greens** (page 190) . . . all of the above . . . **clams** cooked in their shells with olive oil, garlic, and wine . . . leftover **braises**

(Chapter 10) . . . slices of **bacon, lettuce, tomatoes** . . . **aïoli** (page 249), **Pesto** (page 136), or any other **sandwich fillings** . . .

CUTE BUTTERED CROUTONS

Cut ½-inch cubes from close-crumbed white bread, such as brioche, challah, pain de mie, or plain, stale, sliced bread. Toss with melted butter and a little salt. Spread on a baking sheet and toast for 7 minutes (timer!) in a 350°F oven. Toss them around with a spatula and bake for a couple minutes more, if necessary. When they are crisp through and nicely tanned, they're done. Cute croutons, impossible to not snack on, are also for sprinkling on **vegetable soups** (Chapter 8) or **Scrambled Eggs** (page 35) . . . or over **boiled vegetables** (page 171) or **Sautéed Greens** (page 190).

RUSTIC OILY CROUTONS

Carve the crust off of a good rustic loaf with a serrated knife (save the crust, if not too dark, for Crumb 2, page 261) and tear the loaf into 1½-inch pieces. Put them in a bowl, drizzle with olive oil, and sprinkle with a little salt. Toss and repeat until the bread looks coated with oil and tastes good. Spread on a baking sheet and toast for 7 minutes in a 400°F oven. Toss them around with a spatula and bake for a couple minutes more (timer!), if necessary. When they are brown and tan and still soft inside, they're done.

Rustic croutons are for tossing with **salad greens**, especially romaine with Caesar dressing (page 84) . . . making **bread salad** (page 84) . . . sprinkling over braised meats, especially **coq au vin** (page 214) . . . mixing with onions, celery, and herbs and **stuffing** into a chicken before roasting (page 206).

CRUMB 1 (FOR BREADING)

Made by simply crushing or grinding hard, dry bread in a food processor or blender. Use for breading and frying anything. Season, say, **fish fillets** or **skinless, boneless chicken breasts** with salt and pepper. Dust lightly but thoroughly with all-purpose flour, then dip into beaten eggs. Let the excess drip off, and then dredge in Crumb 1 to coat completely. Pan-fry in oil or butter right away, or refrigerate to cook a little later. Crispy-good with tartar sauce (page 249) or aïoli (page 249). I also like to use Crumb 1 to thicken **soups** or to mix into batches of **meat loaf** or **Meatballs** (page 120) or **Fried Green Meat*less*balls** (page 195).

CRUMB 2 (FOR SPRINKLING)

Made with stale bread that still has some give. Carve the crust off of a good rustic loaf with a serrated knife and tear into 1½-inch pieces. A one-pound loaf will yield approximately 4 cups of crumbs. Grind coarsely in a food processor or blender, and then toss in a bowl with plenty of olive oil and a sprinkle of salt. The crumbs should be tasty and pretty oily, though not totally soaked. Spread onto a baking sheet and bake at 350°F for 7 minutes. Using a spatula, scoop the crumbs into a pile, stir them around a bit, and spread them back out. Back into the oven for 5 minutes (timer!) and repeat with the spatula. Keep baking and stirring, resetting the timer each time, until the crumbs are crisp and golden.

Mainly for sprinkling over **pasta**, as you would cheese, oily crumbs can also be used to sprinkle on **chickpeas** or other **beans** (Chapter 3) . . . or **vegetable gratin** (page 240) or **shepherd's pie** (page 166) . . . and will sprinkle the floor as you inevitably snack.

2

EGGS

There used to be an ad campaign from the American Egg Board, a group you don't hear much from anymore—they were fragile, one imagines, and easily beaten. It featured a little jingle: *the incredible, edible egg*. Catchy, and though "edible" sets a low bar by touting what I'd call a minimum requirement, "incredible" perhaps actually *understates* how really amazing, culinarily, eggs are. Rising and falling everywhere from mayonnaise to meringue, eggs are indispensable in kitchens at all levels and fully deserve the praise they so abundantly receive. I won't pile on, but grant me please a moment to say a few words for the common hard-boiled egg. Done right, it is a beautiful and useful thing, not to mention conveniently self-packaged to travel. At home, it can be the addition that makes many a simple dish into a meal, and in fact, significant swaths of my dietary history consisted of little more than halved hard-boiled eggs eaten atop warm beans or toast or both. I still love them that way, though now I'd add a swath of greens. Hard-boiled eggs stand in handsomely as appetizers—think deviled eggs or even simpler: it's amazing how good a platter of halved, properly cooked hard-boiled eggs can look and taste, sprinkled with nothing more than salt, coarse-ground pepper, and some olive oil. When you find yourself desperately in need of entertainment, most kids find it hard not to at least smile when you look them in the eye and crack an egg on your forehead before commencing to peel.

Hard-boiled eggs are perhaps the best picnic food (remember to bring salt and pepper), but on a plane flight, maybe not so good. The perfume of peeling and eating an egg in a confined-air cabin can be misinterpreted, attracting unkind glances. The fried egg sandwich is, I'm afraid, also on the no-fly list. Bananas and granola present no such risks and are better boarding-pass breakfasts.

HARD-BOILED EGGS

Bring a few inches of water to a boil. Add eggs, using a spoon to gently lower them in, and set the timer for 9 minutes (or 8 minutes if you like the yolk a little softer). When done, they can be rinsed in cold water for immediate peeling or left in the shell to peel and eat later. Eggs can be hard to peel, especially if they are very fresh. To ease the operation, tap cooked eggs on the counter to crack the shell all over, and then put them back into the pan with cold water. After 10 minutes they should peel more easily.

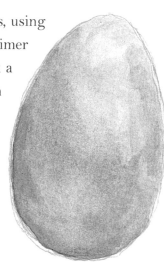

DEVILED EGGS

Cut hard-boiled eggs in half lengthwise and pop out the yolks. Mash them up with salt and pepper and a spoonful of **Mayonnaise** (page 218), or just some **olive oil**. From here you can go in many directions. Minced soft **herbs** are natural to stir in: chives, parsley, mint, cilantro, marjoram, and tarragon. **Chopped celery**, **pickles** (pages 175–76), **capers**, or even **chipotle chilies** are welcome. **Mustard** is classic, and **curry** ought to be. Finely chopped **roasted peppers** (page 183) or mashed **avocado**, or both, can be mixed in. Stuff the yolk mixture back into the whites, but not before they, too, get a sprinkle of salt.

Everyone knows that hard-boiled eggs, and all eggs, are good with toast or tortillas, but there are dozens, many hundreds of dozens, of other ways to

eat them. We like sliced eggs with **beets**, **tomatoes**, or **cucumbers** dressed for a salad with **Red Wine Vinaigrette** (page 83), **Shallot and Sherry Vinaigrette** (page 88), or **Creamy Mustard Dressing** (page 89) . . . ribboned with **anchovy fillets** for a snack on toasts . . . halved on a platter with sliced **pickles** (page 175) of any sort . . . chopped or pushed through a bamboo-handled spider (page 16) and added, with some toasted cumin seeds, to mashed **avocado** to scoop up with chips . . . peeled but left whole and simmered in to boost braised meats, especially in **vindaloo** (page 225) and with **Moroccan spices** (page 215).

The wonderful London chef Sally Clarke reminded me how good simple hard-boiled eggs are when she was cooking a meal with us in Oxford, England, and arrived bearing a clutch of seagull eggs, just enough for an after-work snack for the cooks. Boiled and dipped in celery salt, they were delicious, and though I was relieved that they didn't taste like a seagull's diet of crabs and fish, and believed Sally when she explained how they were sustainably harvested, they *were* foraged from nests in the wild by cliff-climbing egg snatchers, and that felt a little rotten. Like I was Johnny Cash's dirty old egg-sucking dog. Now I use chicken eggs, and apologies to the henhouse, but I feel better this way. To make your own **celery salt**, toast a teaspoon of celery seeds in a small skillet until fragrant. Grind fine in a mortar or spice mill and mix with 5 teaspoons salt. Sprinkle on the hard-boiled eggs of the bird of your choice and/or in Bloody Marys.

POACHED EGGS

In a skillet, bring 2 inches of water to a boil. Crack the eggs into individual cups or small bowls to make it easier to slip them into the water. Season the water with salt and a teaspoon of red or white wine vinegar. Carefully add the eggs, cover the pan, and turn off the heat. Count 5 minutes and dip them out with a slotted spoon. I favor 5-minute poached eggs for the completely set whites and thickened, liquid yolks. If you are more discriminating, bold, brave, and quirky, or want to seem so, go ahead and poach your eggs for 4 minutes and slurp up the soft whites, you beast!

A poached egg can tip a simple dish deep into meal-hood. Peppered and set adrift in a bowl of soup, gently landed in the rough of a sturdy salad, well oiled and awaiting orders in your bowl of beans, a poached egg does what fried and hard-boiled eggs do but with a little more softness, subtlety, and sophistication.

A poached egg fortifies celery soup . . . or any soup.

Lime lifts kedgeree, a leftovers masterpiece.

SCRAMBLED EGGS

Sometimes there's a sweet spot between what's best and what's right. It's not a fixed point; it moves with the moment. Take egg scrambling, for example: there may be a moment when cracking the eggs directly into a hot skillet and then scrambling them in place is that sweet spot, the right, if not best, thing to do, but I honestly can't imagine when that would be— while camping, maybe, or if an earthquake is bringing the walls down around a very hungry you. Even then, I think it would be best to take a breath, gather yourself, and while letting the pan cool some, grab a bowl and stand in the shelter of a doorway while you fork the eggs to a froth. When it's not an earthquake but morning hunger you're trembling with, remember that scrambled eggs are best eaten hot from the skillet, so get your coffee brewed, bacon fried, and toast toasted and buttered before you cook the eggs. Take your time and be sure the skillet is not too hot. Crack the eggs into a bowl large enough to take some action, add salt, crack in pepper, and whisk until completely mixed and streak-free. The butter should foam gently in the skillet; when it stops, add the eggs. Stir slowly, and as soon as they're cooked and set the way you like them, take them out of the skillet so that they don't keep cooking and dry out. Minced soft **herbs** like chives, chervil, or tarragon are a nice addition, and there are times, when you're very hungover maybe, when **cheese** seems like it might be right, but a grind of pepper and a pat of butter are really all the further seasoning required.

Anna, my oldest cooking buddy, turned me on to **kedgeree**, a breakfast masterpiecing of last night's leftovers. I'd never heard of it, though later when doing some research, I learned that you may also know kedgeree as kitcherie, kitchari, kidgeree, kedgaree, or kitchiri. You gotta love a dish with aliases. Kedgeree, as Anna makes it, is a mixture of leftover rice, leftover cooked fish, onions, curry, and scrambled eggs. She made it the morning after a grilled bluefish dinner in a Cape Cod vacation house that our families were sharing. Anna maintains that I am mistaken, that she in fact made it with the more traditional wedges of hard-boiled eggs and not scrambled. I admit that I may misremember, but I like it with scrambled eggs and have cooked it that way ever since. I prefer a flaky mild fish for kedgeree, like cod, halibut, or sole, but it was delicious with assertive bluefish and can be made with whatever you have left over. Heat a skillet to medium and add a couple tablespoons of oil or butter, followed by some diced or sliced onions and a sprinkle of salt. Cook, stirring occasionally, until soft and lightly browned. Add as much curry powder (or any combination of ground cumin, coriander, clove, fennel, black pepper, paprika, cayenne, and turmeric—the turmeric gives curry its distinctive color, so is best not left out) as you like, plus roughly chopped cilantro or parsley, and cook for 30 seconds more. Add a little water and the cooked rice and stir for a couple of minutes, and then break up the fish into the pan. If you have some raisins, especially golden ones, add them in, too. Stir the mixture well and splash in a bit more water if it looks like it's going to get burned before it gets heated through. Turn the heat to low, break some

Scrambling eggs in the midst of kedgeree.

eggs into a bowl, and whisk them up completely. Move the rice mixture to the sides of the skillet, adding a little more butter or oil if things are looking dry, and pour the eggs into the center. Stir gently, and when the eggs are cooked to your liking, either mix everything together and turn out onto a platter or serve as is directly from the skillet. For a more elegant breakfast, scramble the eggs separately and spoon over the rice and fish mixture (or hard-boil, poach, or fry the eggs). Sprinkle with more chopped parsley or cilantro and serve.

Scrambled eggs with sweet summer peppers and tomatoes make up the Basque dish **piperade**. Cook equal parts onions and red peppers, as for peperonata (page 193). Add a third part of chopped tomatoes—peeled and seeded or not—and a little salt, and cook for 5 minutes more. Add whisked-up eggs and cook, stirring occasionally, to your desired doneness. There's great pleasure to be had in the eating of piperade with the best slice of ham you can find.

FRIED EGGS

These are the rules:

1. Heat a skillet, one that won't stick, to low. Use what you must, but well-seasoned cast iron is best. Period.

2. Not too hot. As it is for scrambled eggs, better to start too cool than too hot for a tender fried egg. Add a pat of butter and let it melt, then foam softly, and then add the egg.

3. When the white—all of it—is set, flip the egg, or keep on the sunny side and don't. If an egg sandwich is what you're after, break the yolk before flipping and cook until just set, and your chin will stay unyolked when you bite in.

4. Salt and pepper.

OMELETS

I like a one-egg omelet. A small omelet, I know, but if I'm really hungry, I'd rather eat a hat trick of one-egg omelets than a three-egger any day: the fluffiness of all that egg, lauded in some quarters, has no quarter in my kitchen. Even as a boy I knew this to be true, swirling a thinned and beaten egg in the crepe pan that appeared in my mother's cabinet one day, likely a regifted cast-off, but a breakthrough for me. The crepe-like quality of a modestly stuffed one-egg omelet is precisely where the appeal is.

Serves 1 at a time

1 egg	Freshly ground black pepper
1 tablespoon milk or water	½ tablespoon butter or oil
Salt	Filling of your choice

Crack the egg into a bowl large enough to take some action, add the milk, and season with salt and a crack of pepper. Whisk until completely mixed and streak-free. Heat a skillet just right: the butter should melt, then foam gently. When it stops, add the egg. Tilt the skillet around so the egg swirls to cover it all. When it's set all over with a little liquidy part still in the middle, add the filling to the side you're flipping onto—what will be the bottom of the omelet. For you righties, this is the left side; for lefties, it's the right—this makes for more successful omelet folding. Run a small spatula around the perimeter of the omelet to loosen the edges and then slip it under the unfilled side. Fold it over the filling, turn off the heat, and cover the pan with a lid for a couple of minutes. Take a peek inside, and when it's set the way you like it, tilt the skillet over a plate and use the spatula to slide the omelet out. Hold in a warm oven if you're not eating alone or are already hungry for more and need to make another.

Omelet fillings, family-tested and approved at our house over the years, include **feta cheese**, classic solo or with sliced **scallions** and a few cumin seeds . . . **cheddar** and thin-sliced red, green, or yellow **onion** . . . **goat cheese** and soft fresh **herbs**, such as chives, tarragon, chervil, or mint . . . very thinly sliced **tomatoes** with a spoonful of sour cream and chopped cilantro . . . very thinly sliced tomatoes with a restrained sprinkle of chopped **olives**, **capers**, and **anchovies** (think summer, baguette, rosé) . . . **kimchi** (think winter, rice, tea).

Favorite fillings also include leftovers, and almost any little bit can be a popular candidate: some flakes of cooked **fish** with parsley or pale celery leaves, capers, and a dab of yogurt or sour cream . . . cooked **rice** or **farro**, pan-fried for a minute before you turn the heat to low and add the egg; fold over or leave flat and eat with a **salad** on top . . . strips of braised **pork shoulder**: crisp and brown, set aside, cool the pan, and cook the omelet, filling with the pork, thin avocado slices, scallions, and cilantro . . . **vegetables**, especially **Sautéed Greens** (page 190) or **mushrooms**, cooked any way and chopped, sparingly applied with a little cheese . . . very thinly sliced tomatoes and a spoonful of **Pesto** (page 136) . . . **ratatouille** (page 184) and **ricotta** . . . and, from and for all the line cooks who work hard, stay up late, and wake up hungry: any **leftover Chinese food**, chopped up.

I also like to make flat, unfolded omelets to flip out and let cool, then roll, slice, and eat tossed into **Vegetable Chow Mein–ish** (page 145) or **Singapore shticks** (page 147). Whisk ¼ teaspoon sesame oil and ⅛ teaspoon each salt and sugar with the egg and cook flat, without turning, until the top is set, about a minute.

FRITTATA

For the same reason I like the one-egg omelet, I prefer a frittata to be mostly the filling, with egg providing a supporting structure. To avoid unappealingly dry overfluff, I cook frittatas on the stovetop and never in the oven. It's a little trickier, but it keeps the texture right and the unctuous flavor factor high. Having the filling hot when it's mixed with the eggs helps with the flipping step by sort of cooking the frittata from the inside and avoiding overbrowning the bottom before the center is set.

A frittata tastes good hot, better after it has cooled a half hour or so, and possibly best after it has had a chance to regroup on the countertop for an afternoon. This one is made with a lot of cooked greens and, like all types of frittatas, is great served with a salad of lettuce or raw sliced vegetables, such as fennel, carrots, or radishes, dressed with lemon and olive oil, or a salad of **boiled vegetables** (page 171), such as asparagus or green beans, dressed with Red Wine Vinaigrette (page 83) or Creamy Mustard Dressing (page 89).

---

6 eggs

¼ cup grated Parmesan
  or Pecorino cheese

2 tablespoons olive oil, plus oil or
  butter for the skillet

¼ teaspoon salt

Freshly ground black pepper

1 bunch chard greens, stems torn
  off, washed, chopped, and sautéed
  (page 190)

Heat a skillet over low heat. Crack the eggs into a bowl and whisk very well, until streaks no longer appear. Mix in the cheese, oil, salt, and a grind of pepper. Coat the skillet with a film of oil and add the cooked greens, stirring occasionally until they're heated through. Stir the warm greens into the bowl with the egg mixture.

Return the skillet to medium-low heat. Add a coating of oil or butter and pour in the egg mixture, distributing the greens throughout if they're clumping up. Keep the heat low and rotate the skillet a quarter turn occasionally if the egg seems to be cooking unevenly around the edges. When the perimeter of the frittata looks set and the center is still somewhat liquid, about 8 minutes, run a table knife around the side of the skillet to loosen the frittata and carefully slide a metal spatula under it to loosen the underside.

Invert a plate over the skillet and take the handle in one hand and put the other on the plate. Here comes the exciting part: you're going to flip the frittata onto the plate. I admit that it can end in disaster, but you have to stay confident and strong. You don't want it to slide onto the plate or fold over, so the motion should be up and over, not just over, and it has to happen kind of quickly. Alley-oop, and it's on the plate and the skillet is clean.

Quickly, before the uncooked egg can overrun the plate, film the skillet with a little more oil and, with the help of the spatula, encourage the frittata back in. Don't worry if things are looking a little Humpty Dumpty—just fit it all back together again and continue cooking over low heat. When it's cooked through—make a crack in the middle and

The frittata flip: cover, up, and over . . . success.

sneak a peek to see that the egg is all set—turn the frittata out onto a plate. The good news is that there are two sides to every frittata—if you like the looks of the top side, slide the frittata out the way you slid it in. If you like the looks of the other side better, then flip it out onto a clean plate and show that one. Let cool, slice in wedges or squares, and serve.

Substitute **boiled asparagus** (page 171), cut into 1-inch lengths, for the greens. Chopped fresh **herbs**, such as parsley, basil, chives, mint, or tarragon can be added, and **other boiled green vegetables** (page 171), such as green beans or sweet peas, work well. Little bits of ricotta or goat cheese are nice dabbed into the eggs once in the skillet.

Everyone's favorite at our house is **leftover pasta frittata**.

Start by warming last night's puttanesca, pesto, or primavera—or any other sauced pasta (see Chapters 5 and 6)—in a skillet with a couple tablespoons of water. When it's warm but before it starts to sizzle, stir it into the egg mixture and continue as above. If you have leftover unsauced spaghetti, you can go for a crispier effect: in a couple tablespoons of oil, fry the pasta, spread like a cake. Leave it to get crispy and browned on the bottom, pressing down once or twice on the pasta with a spatula. Turn the heat to low, add the egg mixture—with or without greens—and carry on. Graphically great in uova in trippa (page 45).

My son Milo has only recently come to enjoy exotics like cockscomb, bone marrow, stinging nettles, and the clanking music of Tom Waits. There are some things that you don't like as a kid for what turn out to be the exact reasons you love them later in life: because they're wiggly, sexy, funky, bitter. I myself was confused as a child and young adult by foods like mushrooms, goat cheese, and chicken liver yet envious of their bafflingly genuine appeal to others. Today, of course, they are all—from chicken heads to *Rain Dogs*—delicious. There are, however, still some things that I actively avoid, and tripe is one of them. I've tried and tried and I am sorry, but I will turn in my toque if that's what is required to atone for never having to eat another Moroccan brain salad, kidney pie, or wood oven–braised trippa alla romana. While I await sentencing, please bring me **uova in trippa**, or eggs that look, but do not smell, like tripe: make a marinara sauce (Summer, page 103, or Not-Summer, page 106), maybe a little spicy, and slice some leftover frittata—any kind will do—into thin strips a couple inches long. Toss them gently with the hot marinara and some chopped parsley or basil and serve it to me with grated Parmesan, a garlic-rubbed Thick Soft Toast (page 23), and a glass of Chianti.

3

BEANS

The only kind of beans I ever remember eating as a kid were canned baked beans. Tasting them now, I can see why I liked them then: they're very sweet, too sweet for my taste today, but really, canned beans are okay. They need not be the sugary pork and beans of my youth; good canned organic beans of many types are inexpensive enough and widely available. Still, quality dried beans, when soaked overnight and cooked to creamy tenderness, can be very much better. So good, in fact, that you may just want to eat them plain from a bowl with two glugs of your best olive oil and a sprinkle of salt, and when you do, you will have joined the club that in Tuscany they call *mangiafagioli*, or the bean eaters.

Too often, it must be noted, dried beans don't cook up properly. Half of them are done and starting to break up while the other half are still a little hard. Frequently this is because the beans are too old, and when it happens, you have options: you can just eat them half-done like that, because after cooking for hours, you're hungry now; or you can keep them cooking until they're all soft (and many are beyond soft), and make soup. While you begin a search for better—which most often means fresher—dried beans, you can switch to canned. They're not as good as the best dried but are often better than the worst. To keep your time in the can short, I offer a few favorite varieties from mail-order companies if good dried beans are just not to be found locally:

Rancho Gordo, for borlotti, pinto, and yellow eye beans
(www.ranchogordo.com)

Purcell Mountain Farms, for Christmas lima, black turtle,
and flageolet beans (www.purcellmountainfarms.com)

Phipps Country Store and Farm, for Italian butter cannellini,
French horticultural cranberry, and scarlet runner beans
(www.phippscountry.com)

Beans and pork famously get along. They have a relationship so close that they don't need to always be together. Like the happiest couples, they are each competent and charming on their own yet even more entertaining when together. They just know how to have a good time. Bacon or pancetta, ham of any sort, belly or braise—even if only a scrap, beans don't care.

To bring a sweeter flavor to beans, instead of the pork, or in addition to it, sauté some diced onions, carrot, and celery—the mixture known as mirepoix—with oil and a little salt until completely soft and stir into any type of beans. Lentils, which cook more quickly, can be added into the cooked mirepoix with the water and all cooked together.

BROWN, WHITE, AND RED BEANS

Soak some beans now or as soon as you get home. It will give you a feeling of accomplishment for the next 12 hours; no matter what else you're doing, you're also home cooking. You are a responsible, cleverly frugal, mature individual who knows what he wants for dinner tomorrow night and has the foresight to make it happen. It's therapy with a pulse. Sure, it's geeky, this sort of planning ahead, but in a rustic, chuck-wagon sort of way.

So, look over the dried beans (2½ cups will yield about 6 cups cooked) and pick out any small rocks or dirt clods that may be masquerading as pintos, turtles, or Yankees. Rinse the beans and then put them in a large bowl, cover with plenty of cold water, and leave them overnight on the counter or in the fridge if the weather is hot. Next day, drain the beans, rinse them off a little, and then cover by a couple of inches with fresh water and put them on high heat. Add salt. (Some don't, I do. The simple reason: beans cooked with salt taste better than beans cooked without salt. Flavor trumps.) Then add as many of the following as you have at hand: ½ onion, 1 small carrot, 1 celery stalk, a garlic clove, a bay leaf, a small whole or partial tomato, a thyme sprig or two, parsley stems. These are all just to add flavor and will be discarded in the end, so keep them in big chunks that you can fish out easily. The more of these aromatics you add, the more delicious the beans and their cooking liquid will be. While the best beans will retain their ranking with these additions, the worst will get better.

Can't get anything other than supermarket great northerns or kidneys in dusty plastic bags that look to be past their half-life? Add all of the above and a slice of bacon, more tomato, and a lump of brown sugar and they're nearly back to those baked beans Mom used to make. You could do worse.

Bring the pot of beans to a boil, lower the heat to a simmer, and skim off any foam with a ladle. Taste the water for salt, add more if needed, and cook—stirring infrequently and checking to see if the beans are in need of more water—until very tender but not, hopefully, falling apart. The best-quality beans will achieve this balanced state, but many will not, and it's important to remember that it's not your fault. Blame the bean. Discard the aromatics and leave the beans in the liquid: it keeps them from drying out and can be used for soups.

If you don't want to eat your beans plain from a bowl with two glugs of your best olive oil and a sprinkle of salt like a *mangiafagioli*, that's okay. Save them for later—you can still be in the club. Beans last about 3 days in the refrigerator and freeze well.

BREAD ON BEANS

Preheat the oven to 450°F and put the beans (about ¾ cup per person) in a casserole dish with just enough of the cooking liquid so that the beans on top are on dry land while their brethren below are awash. If it's all seeming too watery, you can mash some of the beans to thicken things up a bit. If the beans are cold, bake them for 15 minutes, then sprinkle oily crumbs (Crumb 2, page 26) on top and bake for another couple of minutes. If the beans are already hot, put the crumbs on from the start and bake away. This is bean gratin and is good straight or with so many things: **Poached Eggs** (page 33) . . . **grilled chicken or meat**, especially sausages (Chapter 11) . . . **Sautéed Greens** (page 190) . . . cut-up and mixed-in **green beans** . . . alongside a couple of slices of summer **tomato**. Of course chopped **herbs**, such as rosemary, sage, marjoram, and thyme, are good mixed into bean gratin.

BEANS ON BREAD 1

Heat a skillet, not too hot, and add a spoonful of olive oil. Fry some rosemary or sage leaves, picked off the stems and very roughly chopped. Add

Tomatoes can be sliced to serve alongside a bean gratin, or chopped and mixed in.

a pinch of crushed red pepper flakes and before anything gets browned at all, add beans and some of their cooking liquid (approximately ¾ cup per person). Let simmer while you toast a thick slice of bread. Rub it with a garlic clove, put it in a bowl, and spoon the hot beans over. Pour on a tablespoon or two of good olive oil. Add an **egg**—fried (page 37), poached (page 33), or hard boiled (page 30)—and, with a little green **salad**, it's a meal.

BEANS ON BREAD 2+

Mash up some beans (about ½ cup per person), without their liquid, in a blender, food processor, or mortar or with a fork in a bowl. Add some pounded garlic, olive oil, and small amounts of finely chopped herbs like rosemary, sage, and/or parsley if you have them. The bean mash should be fairly thick, but if it's too thick and crumbly, stir in a little of the cooking liquid. Spread on Thin Crisp Toast (page 20) for a pre-meal snack. This works well with mediocre beans, better with good beans, and best of all with fresh, late-season fava beans, which, if simmered with a little water and oil, mostly mash themselves.

Make brown or black **bean dip** the same way, but leave out the rosemary, sage, and parsley and use instead toasted and ground cumin seeds (page 11) and either dried oregano or chopped cilantro. If you don't have jalapeños, use crushed red pepper flakes or cayenne. Milo loves bean dip and stirs grated Cheddar or Jack right in, which is good, if goopy. Eat with **tortilla chips** or stuffed in **quesadillas**.

To make **bean salad**, thinly slice a small red onion and put it in a bowl with a couple tablespoons of Red Wine Vinaigrette (page 83) and a sprinkle of salt. Let the onion mellow in the vinaigrette while you see what fresh herbs you have—parsley is good, as is basil, mint, dill, or tarragon, separately or in combinations. Small amounts of oregano, marjoram, sage, or rosemary can work too, chopped very fine. Add the cooled beans, drained of liquid, and stir well. Add more vinaigrette if it seems needed.

You can add a little of the liquid back in if the salad seems too dry. Let sit for 15 minutes and eat, or refrigerate for up to 1 day. **Red or yellow peppers**, raw and thinly sliced or roasted and diced, are good with bean salads, as are diced **tomatoes** and halved cherry tomatoes. Thinly sliced raw **celery** is nice, and **Hard-Boiled Eggs** (page 30), **tuna**, or strips of **anchovies** make bean salad into lunch.

For dinner, make pasta with **Beans and Greens** (page 134).

GREEN LENTILS

Green lentils are perhaps the easiest of dried beans to cook. They don't require soaking, just a rinse, and they cook quickly. Also, unlike browns, yellows, and reds, green lentils don't do that fall-apart thing. Like all beans, green lentils should be cooked just past the stage when they are tender but still chalky: the chalk line. Despite whatever taunts, imagined or real, *do* step over the chalk line, *don't* fall apart, and lentils and life will be that bit better.

1 cup green lentils	½ bay leaf
½ teaspoon salt	1 tablespoon olive oil
1 garlic clove	

Rinse the lentils and put them into a pot with 3 cups of water. Add the salt, garlic, and bay leaf. Bring to a boil, lower the heat to a simmer, and skim any foam. Add the oil and cook the lentils until tender and not chalky, about 30 minutes. Taste for doneness and salt. Eat right away or leave in the liquid to cool for later use.

Some cold day in winter, do yourself a favor and make a nice piece of toast and some **buttered green lentils**. Tip off most of the liquid from cooked lentils (about ¾ cup per person) and set aside. In a small pot

Mix thin slices of raw peppers into lentil or bean salad for color and crunch.

or skillet, bring the lentils to a simmer and add cold slices of butter. Stir, simmering, so that the butter mixes with the lentil liquid as it melts and becomes creamy. Add a little more of the reserved liquid if it's not happening. Add a little more butter if it's raining or really cold out. Taste for salt and add some chopped parsley if you have it. Eat plain with **toast**, with **eggs** and **tomato** wedges, with a couple of boiled **potatoes**, or with **grilled chicken**, **duck**, or **frankfurters**.

Make **green lentil salad** just like bean salad (page 52).

Hummus, or any other mashed beans, makes great platters for sharing.

CHICKPEAS

Chickpeas are heroic in a quiet, quotidian way. Like all beans, chickpeas are humble, but so helpful, so cherubic and cute with their wee queues that you'd forgive them for being a little proud. But no, there they are, uncomplainingly sharing cheap real estate with the hearts of palm and imitation bacon bits on the salad bar, not crushed to be crushed and unheralded in your hummus, not protesting even when they are called peas. They are the one type of bean that seems to consistently cook up properly, even the old supermarket relics. Soaking them with a couple teaspoons of baking soda makes them even more tender.

After soaking, cook the chickpeas as for Brown, White, and Red Beans (page 49). Better overcooked than undercooked for chickpeas (and every bean, really), so be sure to taste several, and if any are still not there, take them over the chalk line.

Chickpeas taste great with **bacon**, **pancetta**, and **sausage**, but I like them especially well with **fish** and **shellfish**. Chickpeas with grilled or roasted **squid** and **aïoli** (page 249) are as delicious as they are economical. Grilled fish or shrimp are maybe happiest tucked under **Salsa Verde** (page 244) on a bumpy bed of chickpeas. Clams steamed open with garlic, crushed red pepper flakes, and a little water or white wine will often embrace a ladleful of warm chickpeas, holding them in their shells like plump golden pearls.

A **salad** of cool chickpeas, dressed like bean salad (page 52), is even better dressed with slices of hard-boiled egg (page 30) and strips of anchovies.

Hummus is, of course, simply mashed chickpeas, with or without tahini. A blender or food processor will make it smooth, but a mortar and pestle or even a bowl and fork will work. Drain the chickpeas and save the cooking liquid. Crush them however you choose and then add pounded garlic, salt, lemon juice, olive oil, and tahini if you are using it. Add some of the cooking liquid if the hummus seems too thick. Taste and add more of whatever is needed, remembering that the garlic flavor will grow over time. Hummus is good on pita or crackers but also nice just spread thickly on a plate, doused with olive oil, and topped with a crunchy little salad dressed simply with lemon and olive oil, such as thinly sliced raw fennel or radishes or artichokes or celery or peppers; sliced tomatoes and cilantro; cherry tomatoes and chunky cucumbers; arugula and mint leaves. Sumac, the deep red, lemony Middle Eastern spice, looks and tastes wonderful sprinkled on hummus and so many salads. A jar of ground sumac can be mail-ordered if you can't find it at your market.

In winter, mix equal parts hummus and roasted and mashed hard **squash** (page 180). In autumn, for a pumpkiny glow, toasted and crushed cumin seeds and a little cayenne.

Bean Soups

All beans make great soup, and some are so eager that they seem to make themselves into soup even when you don't want them to. Dried white beans with which one was hoping to make a salad turn out to be too old—disappointing and dissolving despite proper soaking and a well-tended simmer; red lentils, meanwhile, spontaneously self-simmer to pieces, and one is grateful. Soup is what they both can easily become, and a considered addition of rosemary and garlic to the former, or a confident dose of curry spices to the latter, and they'll be soups worth making again.

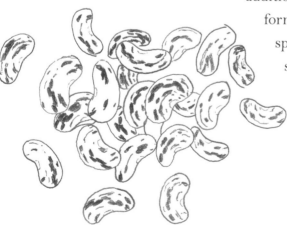

BROWN, YELLOW, OR RED LENTIL DAL

These lentils are soup magic. Neither the magic that makes a beanstalk to the clouds nor the magical fruit of song, theirs is a magic of transformation: now discrete lentil entities, now a unified soup. This soup, Indian dal, is always delicious, often auspicious, and good to eat every day. I like it best served in small bowls to start a meal, but it can be a meal in itself spooned over plain white or brown rice with a side of **boiled** (page 171) or **roasted** (page 179) **vegetables** or **Sautéed Greens** (page 190).

---

3 tablespoons olive oil

1 medium yellow onion, diced

1 teaspoon salt

1 tablespoon crushed whole
  cumin seeds

1 tablespoon crushed whole
  coriander seeds

1 teaspoon crushed whole fennel
  seeds

½ teaspoon crushed red pepper
  flakes

1 tablespoon ground turmeric

2 cups lentils, rinsed

3 tablespoons butter or oil
  (optional)

1 teaspoon garlic, minced
  (optional)

½ teaspoon dried mint (optional)

Yogurt (optional)

Chopped mint or cilantro
  (optional)

Heat a soup pot over high heat. Add the oil and then the onions and salt. Stir, turn the heat to low, and cover the pot. Check and stir after a few minutes, letting the moisture on the lid drip back into the pot to keep things steamy. Lower the heat if there is any browning going on, and re-cover. Cook like this until the onion is tender, about 15 minutes. Add the cumin, coriander, fennel, and red pepper flakes and cook, stirring, for 1 minute to toast the spices. Add the turmeric and stir for 30 seconds more. Add the lentils and 4 cups water and bring to a boil. Lower the heat to a simmer and cook, stirring occasionally, until the lentils give up their earthly bodies and become one with your dinner, about 30 minutes. If you want the dal to be smoother, you can just stir the heck out of it, pass it through a food mill, or even spin it in the blender, though I usually find these steps unnecessary.

Often, a "sizzle" of butter with garlic and more of the spices is made and spooned over the bowls of dal. To make a sizzle, heat a small saucepan, add oil or butter, and when it's hot, add the garlic and more of the spices you used in the soup. Let it sizzle for 30 seconds till it smells really good and then spoon it over the dal. Dried mint, as for tea, is also a nice addition to a sizzle.

Put a spoonful of **plain yogurt** on each bowl of dal. Sprinkle with chopped cilantro or mint.

BLACK BEAN SOUP

3 tablespoons olive or
 vegetable oil

1 large red onion, diced

½ teaspoon salt

1 tablespoon toasted cumin seeds

½ teaspoon crushed red pepper
 flakes

4 garlic cloves, sliced or chopped

1 strip orange peel

6 cups cooked black turtle beans,
 with their liquid (2½ cups dried)

1 quart water, chicken stock
 (page 206), or pork stock
 (page 222)

¼ teaspoon dried oregano

Sour cream (optional)

Chopped cilantro (optional)

Scallions (green and white parts),
 chopped, to taste (optional)

Lime (optional)

Heat a soup pot over high heat and add the oil, all but a couple tablespoons of the diced red onion (for garnish), and the salt. Stir in the cumin and red pepper flakes, turn the heat to low, and cover the pot. Check and stir after a few minutes, letting the liquid on the lid drip back into the pot to keep things steamy. Lower the heat if there is any browning going on, and re-cover. Cook like this until the onion is tender, about 15 minutes, and then add the garlic and orange peel, raise the heat to high, and stir for half a minute, until fragrant. Add the beans and their cooking liquid and the water. Bring to a boil and then lower the heat to a simmer. Crumble in the oregano and cook until the flavors all come together, about 30 minutes. Taste and add more cumin, red pepper flakes, garlic, or oregano if you like. Eat the soup just like this, or put it in a blender or through a food mill for a very smooth effect. Sometimes it's nice to grind up some of the beans to thicken the soup but leave most of them intact.

To bring light to the delicious darkness of black bean soup, add (if desired) a spoonful of sour cream and some chopped cilantro, the reserved red onion diced or chopped, scallions, and a squeeze of lime to your bowl.

PASTA E CECI

Make this soup just like you would Crema di Fagioli (page 68), but with chickpeas, naturally, and grinding not all but just about a third of them to return to the pot. Separately, boil some pasta and put a small handful in each bowl and ladle the hot soup over. Garlicky Sautéed Greens (page 190) are welcome, chopped and added to either the pot or the bowl. If there's that bottle of very good olive oil on your shelf, this soup will let it shine. Make this with white beans instead of chickpeas and it is the charmingly named pasta fazool.

LEBLEBI

This North African soup combines a simple stew of onion, cilantro, and spiced chickpeas with toasted bread chunks, turning humble to sublime, especially if you set a poached or hard-boiled egg on top. Liam and I like it for a satisfying after-school snack, even for 2 or 3 days running. I put a spoonful of spicy harissa and a sprinkle of capers on mine. Liam takes his straight. We try to say "We love leblebi!" three times fast, with full mouths and true hearts.

4 tablespoons olive or vegetable oil

1 large yellow onion, diced

1 teaspoon salt

2 teaspoons cumin seeds

1 teaspoon paprika

Crushed red pepper flakes

½ cup roughly chopped cilantro stems and leaves

2 garlic cloves, sliced or chopped

¾ cup chopped or grated tomatoes or ½ cup roasted tomato puree (page 184)

6 cups cooked chickpeas, with their liquid (2½ cups dried)

Small handful of Rustic Oily Croutons (page 25) per bowl

1 poached (page 33) or hard-boiled (page 30) egg per bowl

Ground cumin (optional)

Good-quality extra-virgin olive oil (optional)

Capers (optional)

Harissa sauce (opposite; optional)

Heat a soup pot over high heat. Add the oil, then the onion and salt. Stir, lower the heat, and cover the pot. Check and stir after a few minutes, letting the liquid on the lid drip back into the pot to keep things steamy. Lower the heat if there is any browning going on, and re-cover. Cook like this until the onion is tender, about 15 minutes. Add the cumin, paprika, red pepper flakes, cilantro, and garlic and stir for 1 minute. Add the tomatoes to stop the garlic from browning and cook for a couple minutes more, stirring occasionally. Add the chickpeas and enough of their cooking liquid to cover by 2 inches, raise the heat, and bring to a boil. Lower to a simmer and cook for 20 minutes. Put 2 ladles of soup in a blender or food mill and puree (careful—it's hot). Return to the soup pot and stir in to thicken the leblebi slightly. Taste for seasonings and add water or any reserved cooking liquid if it's too thick.

To serve, put some croutons in each soup bowl. Ladle in the leblebi and top with a poached egg or a halved hard-boiled egg. Sprinkle with a little ground cumin and oil and capers if you like, and pass a bowl of harissa sauce to spoon over at the table.

Tubes of prepared **harissa**, like some kind of practical joke toothpaste, can be found at Middle Eastern markets. At Asian markets, I buy sambal oelek—the chili paste that comes in a little jar with a green top and a gold label with a red rooster on it—and make a quick harissa by stirring 3 tablespoons of it with 1 or more pounded garlic cloves and 6 tablespoons olive or vegetable oil.

For a more nuanced harissa sauce, mix 2 tablespoons paprika or any other mild chili powder with enough hot water to make a thick paste, about 3 tablespoons. Stir in 2 teaspoons pounded garlic and 3 tablespoons olive or vegetable oil. I often want a splash of red wine vinegar in there and sometimes will add some ground cumin, and cayenne if it needs heating up. A tablespoon or two of currants or raisins, plumped for 10 minutes in hot water, adds a sweet counterpoint.

SPLIT PEA WITH HAM OR BACON (AND DON'T YOU MAKE IT WITHOUT!)

Oh, all right, I guess you can make it without . . . for your friend who might be vegan or keeping to rules. The peas are meaty enough, but I'd miss the smokiness. It's a long haul for such a nor'easter of a soup, but a Mexican chipotle or other smoked, mild chili could make the trip.

3 tablespoons vegetable or light olive oil

1 yellow onion, diced

1 carrot, diced small

2 celery stalks, diced small

2 teaspoons salt

A ham bone, smoked hock, ½ cup chopped ham or bacon, or 1 or 2 chopped chipotle chilies

1 bay leaf

2 cups split peas, about a pound

6 cups water or pork stock (page 222)

1 pat of butter per bowl (optional)

Small handful of Cute Buttered Croutons (page 25) per bowl (optional)

Freshly ground black pepper

Heat a soup pot over high heat. Add the oil and then the onion, carrot, celery, and 1 teaspoon of the salt. Stir, lower the heat, and cover the pot. Check and stir after a few minutes, letting the liquid on the lid drip back into the pot to keep things steamy. Lower the heat if there is any browning going on, and re-cover. Cook like this until the vegetables are very tender, about 20 minutes. Uncover and add the ham bone and bay leaf. Stir and add the peas, water, and the remaining teaspoon of salt and turn up the heat. Stir occasionally as the soup comes to a boil, and then lower to a simmer. Stirring from time to time, cook until the peas are starting to fall apart and have lost any chalkiness, about 45 minutes.

If desired, set 1 pat of butter on each bowl of soup and sprinkle with croutons. Add a generous grinding of pepper. Feel the comfort.

RIBOLLITA

Like many soups, ribollita and her summer cousin, pappa al pomodoro, just keep on getting better as they age. Ribollita is good the day you make it and great the next and the next for about 4 days. I once served ribollita in the kitchen of a Chianti villa at midnight to a very pregnant Italian opera singer and her hovering mother. I was in the middle of a weeklong cooking gig in Italy, and the soup was a good batch, thick and doused with some fresh, local olive oil, and the hungry post-performance diva was sated and impressed. Her doting mother was impressed, too, but skeptical, unconvinced that I, *un americano*, had actually made the soup, despite clear evidence—my position at the stove, the ladle in my hand, the stains on my apron! I was as proud as a new dad.

---

3 tablespoons olive oil

1 yellow onion, diced

1 carrot, diced small

2 celery stalks, diced small

1½ teaspoons salt

2 garlic cloves, chopped

Chopped leaves from 1 rosemary or sage sprig, or chopped leaves from ½ sprig each

½ cup chopped tomato

1 bunch lacinato (or other) kale, leaves stripped from the stems, washed, drained, and chopped

6 cups chicken stock (page 206) or water

2½ cups cooked white or brown beans, with their liquid (1 cup dried)

½ loaf stale bread, torn or chopped into chunks

Your best extra-virgin olive oil

Heat a soup pot over high heat. Add the oil and then the onion, carrot, celery, and 1 teaspoon of the salt. Stir, lower the heat, and cover the pot. Check and stir after a few minutes, letting the liquid on the lid drip back into the pot to keep things steamy. Lower the heat if there is any browning going on, and re-cover. Cook like this until the vegetables are very tender, about 20 minutes. Uncover and add the garlic and rosemary. Stir for a couple minutes, raise the heat, and add the tomato. Cook, stirring occasionally, for a few minutes, and then add the kale, the remaining ½ teaspoon salt, and the stock. Add the beans, turn the heat to high, and bring to a low boil. Lower the heat to keep the soup at a simmer and cook for another 20 minutes. Turn off the heat, add the bread, and stir well. Let the ribollita sit for at least 15 minutes (or up to 5,760 minutes) before eating with lots of your best olive oil poured over.

Ribollita really does gain something from being allowed to cool, then reheated. The name, meaning "reboiled," refers to this. If your ribollita is very thick the next day, you can thin it a little, or if it's very solid, slice off a slab instead to pan-fry for the best crusty, molten lunch.

Leave out the bread and this is **minestrone**. In the summer, we add more tomato and small diced zucchini, peppers, and green beans, and serve with a spoonful of basil **Pesto** (page 136). In winter, we might use hard squash, celery root, and parsnip with a pesto of parsley and marjoram or oregano. Spring: spinach, peas, and asparagus with a mint pesto. Little pasta shapes are cute in minestrone. Boil them separately and add only to the soup you are going to eat right away, or they get soft and squishy.

Hot minestrone activates pesto or other garlicky green sauces.

CREMA DI FAGIOLI

Ignore the name, which translates to "bean cream"—a charm-free title that at least sounds better in Italian, as do so many things, *amore mio*—the beauty of this soup is in its velvety texture. A countertop blender, an immersion blender, or a food processor works best to summon the crema. A hand-cranked food mill does fine as well.

---

3 tablespoons olive oil

1 yellow onion, sliced

1 small carrot, peeled and sliced

1 teaspoon salt

2 garlic cloves, chopped

Crushed red pepper flakes

Scant tablespoon chopped rosemary and/or sage leaves

¾ cup roasted tomato puree (page 184) or grated tomato (optional)

6 cups cooked brown, white, or red beans, with their liquid (2½ cups dried)

2 cups water, chicken stock (page 206), or pork stock (page 222)

Freshly ground black pepper

Your best extra-virgin olive oil or 1 pat of butter per bowl (optional)

Heat a soup pot over high heat. Add the oil and then the onion, carrot, and salt. Stir, lower the heat, and cover the pot. Check and stir after a few minutes, letting the liquid on the lid drip back into the pot to keep things steamy. Lower the heat if there is any browning going on, and re-cover. Cook like this until the onion is tender, about 15 minutes. Add the garlic, red pepper flakes, and rosemary. Stir for 1 minute and then add the tomato puree (if using) and cook for a couple minutes more. Add the beans and their liquid, turn up the heat, and give the pot a good stir. The beans should be covered by about 1 inch with liquid. If they're not, add some water. Everything is cooked already, so you just need to simmer for 15 to 20 minutes for the flavors to come together. Carefully blend, process, or mill the soup in batches and return it to the pot. Add a generous grinding of pepper, stir, and taste, adding more of what's needed and thinning with water if still too thick.

If the cooked beans are unlovely in appearance or lacking in flavor, using the optional tomato can really help.

If desired, finish each bowl with a drizzle of oil.

4

SALAD DRESSINGS AND WHAT TO DRESS

My mother had a Tupperware "salad crisper" that looked like a lime-green iceberg, with a soft snap-on top and a spiky pedestal upon which the uncrisp was to be impaled. Though it was nominally available for storage of salad in general, it was clearly intended for one type in particular. I remember Mom smacking a pale, impassive iceberg lettuce on our kitchen counter before tearing out its dangling heart and fitting that green spike into the hole left in its heavy head. This was clearly a lettuce for which some serious mom handling was nothing—nothing that a couple of days in the crisper wouldn't fix, that is.

Later, I would stand in the open doorway of the fridge and, fueled by teenage after-school hunger, tear chunks of iceberg from the resident head, mixing them with bottled Wishbone French and anything, everything, I could find. I'd slice in vegetables like cucumbers, scallions, cherry tomatoes, and green peppers, adding bouncy cubes of Jarlsberg cheese, too-salty Pepperidge Farm croutons that started stale and stayed there, and shameless shakes from a bottle of those meat-impersonator washups, Bac-Os.

Though the good folks at Tupperware might wish it otherwise, there may be no lettuce less in need of crisping than iceberg—indeed, crispness seems to be its defining characteristic, its sole virtue, and it's certainly the reason that I remain an enthusiast. But there are green gardens far beyond iceberg's watery world: salads leafy with rockets, cresses, herbs, butters, and Bibbs; others crunchy with shavings of carrots, fennel, radishes, and cucumbers. Roasted beets, boiled green beans, grilled asparagus . . . it goes on for acres.

All three of our sons have always liked eating salads, or at least they like eating vegetables raw rather than cooked. Milo was especially herbivorous as a boy, chomping like a hungry, hungry caterpillar through snap peas, asparagus stalks, and celery but also whole fava bean pods, entire unpeeled mangos, and fistfuls of wild green onions that flowered along our walk and made his breath stink in a sweaty green way that inspired us to create a self-serving stipulation: wild onion eating only on the way to school, never on the way home. Sorry, Teacher.

Later, having graduated to more conventional salad appreciation, Milo and his brothers liked best a dressing that was a favorite of mine as well: egg and anchovy. Considerably less pungent than Milo's wild onions, but still, it wasn't one that I expected to be tolerated, let alone requested. We started eating it on sweet lettuces like romaine and butter, and when I began tossing in bitters like escarole and radicchio and heard no complaints, I knew a new leaf had turned in our family diet. True, young Liam still prefers his the same way I order mine when eating out and wary of the kitchen's abilities—dressing on the side, please—but it was clear: the salad days had dawned.

When my wife and I are slowed down with friends at home and want an in-between pause to talk or tend to children, we sometimes like to have a cooked vegetable salad of asparagus, green beans, maybe beets, and take our time before eating the pasta or roasted chicken. Leafy salads are good

like that, too, but also served right alongside the meat of the meal, or even right after, to lighten things up. While most salads should be dressed immediately before serving or risk wilting, there are those, like coleslaw and other raw, sliced vegetable salads, that benefit from some time spent dressed—marinating and becoming tender.

dressing staples

Beautiful lettuces and vegetables can be spoiled by a bad dressing, it's true, but regular produce—even lesser stuff—can be if not rescued, then at least thrown a line by a really good one. As foliated as they often are, salads nevertheless offer scant camouflage to hide behind: there's little or no cooking to roast away flaws and caramelize flavors, so the ingredients have to be especially sweet and fresh. The tastiest dressing can offer savory solace, but as it is still the sum of its handful of parts, here are some tips on finding tasty parts.

OLIVE OIL

In Greece, Italy, France, and Spain, you can hardly cut a slice off a crusty rustic loaf without your elbow knocking over a bottle of great olive oil— fresh, green, and peppery. If you travel there, I recommend you eat lots of it—for pleasure and, some say, longevity. Here in the United States, where supermarket shelves are lousy with decidedly un-great oils and doors to fancier stores are blocked by budget limits, it's not so easy, and the best choice for an olive oil can often be the one that tastes least. Too many extra-virgin oils that should taste fruity like a green olive instead taste fruity like an old yellow crayon. Coloring dinner with that shade is not pretty—better to get oil that's more food-toned. If that means buying light olive oil, which, though it perhaps doesn't contribute a lot of flavor, also doesn't get in the way, then so be it.

When you do find that great olive oil, don't save it. It's not like wine— it doesn't get better with age. Like all of us, oil begins to perish the moment it is squeezed from the source. The mother of a very good chef- friend told me that when she was first married, someone gave her a fancy bottle of olive oil, and over the years, when she cooked with it on special occasions, she remembered being surprised by its curious flavor. Recently, after having tasted good, fresh olive oil at her son's place, she realized that her old, special oil, which had seemed so perplexingly exotic, was simply rancid. It doesn't have to be like that: if you somehow find yourself fixed with a bottle of newly pressed peppery olive oil when it comes green to markets in November and December (whether a splurge purchase, a gift, or through unctuous larceny, lucrative employment, or a spontaneous trip to Alicante or Lucca, I don't need to know), pour it on, spoon it up, wipe your chin, and eat it all by April.

Olive oil is best within a year of production, so check dates when buying and use it up within 6 months from when you open it. Taste the oil before you buy it, if possible; otherwise, buy in the smallest size bottle or tin, and if you like it, get more next time. There are good and great oils from Italy, France, Spain, and Greece, of course, but do not overlook some of the fine olive oils being made in California. Among many others, I like to cook with the oils from Katz Farm (www.katzandco.com) and Casa Rosa Farm (www.casarosafarm.com).

VINEGAR

Balsamic vinegar has virally colonized the American kitchen. Maybe it's the sweetness or the rich, dark color that has us enthralled and enslaved, but it seems to be everywhere. I'm not saying that you should dump your bottle, just that balsamic should not be the go-to vinegar that it has so insidiously become. The real go-to is red wine vinegar, and it's high time it takes its rightful place in the front row of your pantry. Other useful, but not necessary, vinegars to have on hand for dressings are sherry, white wine or champagne, and yes, that monster from Modena, the megaloma-niacal *balsamico*.

GARLIC, MUSTARD, AND LEMON

Happily, these are three common dressing ingredients that are easy to find in good quality. The garlic will be used raw here, so get the best, and freshest you can find. In the spring, look for green garlic. It looks like a slender leek—the bulb hasn't formed yet—and you can use the whole thing and in just the same way that you'd use bulb garlic. Bulb garlic is sent to markets in the summer and, when dried and stored properly, will last until the next year; garlic that you're buying in the winter is many months out of the ground and only getting stronger. Use less and look forward to the new crop. If you don't already have a favorite Dijon-type mustard, Maille and Grey Poupon are good standbys. And it's our sunny good fortune, for which we will no doubt one day have to pay, that lemons are pretty much always in markets.

ANCHOVIES

As delicious as big fishes like tuna, salmon, and swordfish are, instead of eating *them*, it's probably better that we eat *like* them and cook more often with tasty little fishes, like anchovies. Unless you can get your mouth around a whole school, tuna-style, anchovies themselves don't make a meal, but they can make one better. Good anchovies, whether salt- or oil-packed, are like a tiny umami tsunami of salty and sweet but, once opened, remain delicious for only a day or two. After that, they get fishier and take on a metallic, oxidized flavor that may have a lot to do with why anchovies are popularly misunderstood and reviled in this country. I buy the smallest cans or jars I can find (Agostino Recca makes very good ones), cook with what I need, and either make a plan for using the remainder the next day or make like a top predator and have a snack.

the undressed

Despite what you may have heard or the hurry you're in, salad greens need to be washed, because it's unpleasant to crunch on grit. The other reason to wash salad greens is that a dip in cold water gives them a freshening lift, a crisping. Once washed, dry them so that the dressing will stay strong and stick to the leaves.

Some of our favorite salads are made of raw, thinly sliced, crunchy vegetables. They make the adults feel healthy and happy and the kids just happy. I most often perform the business part of slicing these salads with nothing more than a knife, but my skills are sharpened and so are my knives. If yours are not so, there are many devices for slices. Razor-bladed planers known as mandolines are popular, but I find the pushing-the-fingers-at-the-blade aspect too perilous. If you use one, turn off the music, clear the room of distractions, and focus your brain as if for per-

forming salad surgery. A humbler, safer technique I prefer is to subvert the common cheese planer, that thing that looks like a little spatula with a slot. Hold the vegetable in place on your cutting board by spearing it with a fork so that fingers are not endangered, and slice it into thin sheets with the cheese planer, or cheese wangler, as we call it at home. Small zucchini, sliced lengthwise, transcend themselves cut this way, and I have even cut potato chips with the wangler. The large holes of a box grater are also useful for making shredded salads. To get longer, prettier strips of carrots, cucumbers, or zucchini, hold them vertically, nearly parallel to the surface of the grater, and use long strokes.

For cooked vegetable salads, boil them in abundant, well-salted water. The water should be, and remain, at a vigorous boil, so cook the vegetables in batches if necessary. The only way to know when they are done is to taste them after a few minutes to see if they are tender enough, then dip them out and spread them on a plate to cool. I prefer to not plunge them into cold water after cooking—what may be gained in color retention does not offset the loss in flavor. Unless you are saving the cooked vegetables for much later, there's no need to refrigerate them; they taste better at room temperature.

dressing-room gear

The ingredients of Stone Age salads were likely more bark and bush than rocket and romaine, but paleo-vinaigrettes must have been made with stone implements that still serve us perfectly today: a mortar and pestle. Blenders and spice mills have made crushing and grinding easier, if noisier, but the ancient team of M&P remains unbeatable for grinding toasted spices, making herb sauces and aïoli (page 249), pounding garlic, smashing anchovies, and—salads rejoice!—mixing vinaigrettes. Ceramic mortars and pestles I cannot recommend; though pretty, their clinking porcelain surfaces are too wincingly dental for me. Much better are heavy stone mortars, whose pestles easily grind spices to dust or anchovies to paste. Dear to my hearth are two wooden models, one of which, my first, now sits ready and awaiting orders on Henderson's kitchen shelf. The other is a fine-grained beauty that fits snugly in hand at home and grinds its olive-wood heart out for us.

Even dads know that babies wet from the bath need drying before dressing. Salad greens are like that. Layered with paper towels, slung aloft in a pillowcase, or strung on threads with tiny clothespins—however you need to get it done. I like a spinner with a string pull myself (for the salad, not the babe).

Proper dressing of a salad must be done with your hands. Tongs or forks simply cannot ensure thorough but gentle coating with dressing the way our most useful tools can. Get a friend to sprinkle in more of what's needed when your hands get too slippery.

LEMON AND OLIVE OIL DRESSING

Salad greens like arugula, cress, and baby lettuces are often best dressed with nothing more than salt and pepper, a squeeze of lemon juice, and a splash of nice olive oil. No need to mix up a dressing separately, just add each ingredient to the bowl of salad and toss with your hands to coat well. Taste and add more of whatever is needed.

Thinly sliced **raw fennel**, **celery**, **radishes**, or **little turnips** in spring are very good this way, with or without some chopped parsley or mint.

Grated or thinly sliced **raw carrots** are more exotic tasting than you thought common carrots could be with lime replacing the lemon and the addition of toasted cumin seeds and a little cayenne pepper.

Raw zucchini one way: thinly sliced with lemon and oil, salt and pepper, chopped mint and parsley. Toss all together, spread out on a plate, and top with shavings or gratings of Parmesan or Pecorino cheese and a little handful of toasted pine nuts (page 11).

Raw zucchini another way: thinly sliced with thinly sliced cucumbers, lime and oil, salt and pepper, cilantro and grated ginger. Toss all together, spread out on a plate, and top with a little handful of toasted pine nuts (page 11).

RED WINE VINAIGRETTE

Of course garlic can and should be added to lemon and olive oil dressing or any other dressing, but it perhaps feels most at home in a red wine vinaigrette. Pungent vinegar embraces and calms pungent garlic whether it is mashed to a pulp with a pinch of salt or just a cracked clove sunk in the mix. This is the beloved dressing at home, daily and dearly, and everyone in the family makes it. Personal variations have emerged based on flavor preferences, scarcity of one or more ingredients, and enthusiasm levels: sometimes, it's true, even pounding some garlic can be more than we're able to muster. And speaking of mustard, when the jar is empty and has been thoroughly dredged, and if there are not too many crumbs or smears of ketchup in there, we pour in some red wine vinegar, salt, pepper, a cracked garlic clove, and olive oil; screw the cap on; and shake. If it's too mustardy, in goes more oil and maybe a shot more vinegar; more shaking, and we have dressing for days.

½ to 1 small garlic clove, either pounded with salt or simply cracked once with the side of a knife

⅛ teaspoon salt

Freshly ground black pepper

2 teaspoons red wine vinegar

½ teaspoon Dijon mustard (optional)

3 tablespoons good olive oil

Mix the garlic, salt, pepper, vinegar, and mustard (if using) together in a small bowl or jar with a lid. Stir the olive oil into the bowl or add to the jar and shake. Vigorously stir or shake the vinaigrette to blend completely just before dressing the salad. If you used a whole, cracked garlic clove, take it out after 10 minutes or up to 2 hours and discard it.

Red wine vinaigrette works every leafy time, especially on **little mixed lettuces** or **arugula**.

In late summer, when the tomatoes are sweet and so juicy that they need some bread like tonic needs gin, cut them into chunks along with cucumbers and toss with Rustic Oily Croutons (page 25) for **bread salad**. Basil, mint, and parsley are obvious joiners, as are scallions or vinaigrette-marinated thin slices of raw red onions. Grate in an extra tomato or sprinkle in a little water if the salad needs to be juicier. In tomatoes' long off-season, keep the herbs and onions in there and add sautéed or boiled and chopped kale, sliced and boiled celery, or even some pickled vegetables (page 175). I have left out the bread itself and made a similar salad with boiled farro or leftover rice.

EGG AND ANCHOVY DRESSING

Caesar is probably the best-known version of this dressing. A dear old friend—a hard-living, bighearted private investigator and avid eater—liked making Caesar dressing a lot. Maybe it was the coddling of the egg that he felt especially expert at, but more likely it was the opportunity to slurp up a few anchovy fillets on the side as he shook in the Tabasco and Worcestershire and drank glasses of cold vodka. I don't always take egg and anchovy dressing to the empire of Caesar, but when I do, I pour a drink and think of Bobby.

1 garlic clove, pounded with a pinch of salt to yield about ½ teaspoon	1 tablespoon red wine vinegar
	Freshly ground black pepper
6 anchovy fillets (half of a 2-ounce can or jar)	1 raw egg yolk or 1 whole egg, boiled for 8 minutes and chopped
1 teaspoon Dijon mustard	6 tablespoons olive oil
1 teaspoon lemon juice	

Mash the garlic and anchovies together, either in a mortar with the pestle or on a cutting board with a knife. Add the mustard, lemon juice, vinegar, and pepper to the mortar (or place them in a bowl with the garlic and anchovies) and stir to mix well. Add the egg yolk and then stir in the olive oil. If you want the dressing to be thick and creamy, pour the olive oil in a thin stream as you stir spiritedly with the pestle or a whisk as for mayonnaise. (It has always struck me as absurd that the pestle and the whisk, one so singular and the other so multiple, create emulsions equally well. Surely there's some kind of science at work here, but I just love the magic.) Use egg and anchovy dressing today or by tomorrow at the latest.

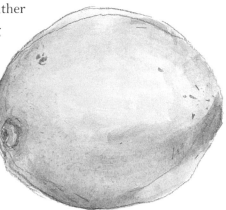

Dress lettuces like **butter, romaine, iceberg,** or **radicchio** with egg and anchovy dressing. **Belgian endive** is great with it, and when thin slices of raw vegetables like **fennel, turnips, radishes,** or **Jerusalem artichokes** are likewise dressed, they have been known to make converts of professed anchovy and vegetable haters.

Cooked asparagus, artichokes, and cauliflower, warm or cool, warm to it.

If you just must, leave out the anchovies. We do it often, actually, usually because we ran out, but with a little extra mustard, the dressing is still very good. Anchovy and Bacon aren't particularly good friends themselves, but both get along well with Egg and most often can successfully stand in for each other. Were I ever to revisit vegetarianism, I'd be the kind who eats no meat other than anchovy and bacon. Anchoconians? Bacovians? You know who you are, stand up!

Grated Parmesan cheese is all it takes to make this into **Caesar dressing**.

Egg and anchovy dressing has the power to convert even kids into vegetable admirers.

Although my friend Bobby felt the coddling of the egg to be essential to the success of Caesar, I don't see it. I just start with a raw egg yolk, mix in the other ingredients, and very slowly whisk in the oil, like for Mayonnaise (page 248). The black pepper gives all the heat necessary, so I skip the Tabasco, but when I'm feeling nostalgic for my old best friend's cooking, I'll shake in a little Worcestershire. **Rustic Oily Croutons** (page 25) are recommended, if not required, and are best dressed in with the romaine, so they soften a little. **Escarole**, **endive**, and **frisée** all taste great with Caesar dressing, as does a **salad** of thinly sliced celery, either raw or briefly boiled and cooled.

Salad dressing served warm and made with butter? Leave it to the Italians to make, and then break, the rules. **Bagna cauda**, meaning "warm bath," is a bowl of warm garlic and anchovy dressing around which lucky eaters gather to dip slices of raw vegetables. Communal mess-making gets a dinner going like nothing else can. We encourage guests to hold a piece of bread beneath the bathed vegetable for its journey mouthward, catching drips of the dip and becoming a tasty bite in its own right—an edible blotter. Mash 2 large garlic cloves and 12 anchovy fillets together, either on a cutting board with a knife or in a mortar with the pestle. Over low heat, melt 1 tablespoon butter with 2 tablespoons olive oil. Add the garlic and anchovy mixture and cook very slowly, stirring and mashing the anchovies occasionally, until it all melts together and smells really good, about 15 minutes. Serve bagna cauda warm, right from the pan or in little cups or bowls, with slices of the best raw vegetables of the season for dipping and a loaf of bread for protection.

SHALLOT AND SHERRY VINAIGRETTE

We love to eat well-dressed salads of hearty greens on the same plate as roasted chicken (Chapter 9) or braised pork (page 222) or duck legs (page 219). This simple vinaigrette makes especially good company for meats of all sorts, the sherry vinegar mixing politely with the juices while the pickle-y shallots contribute pungent and acidic asides.

---

1 small shallot	1 teaspoon sherry vinegar
Good pinch of salt (about ⅛ teaspoon)	½ teaspoon Dijon mustard
1 teaspoon red wine vinegar	Freshly ground black pepper
	3 tablespoons olive oil

Peel and mince the shallot in a tiny imitation of dicing an onion (page 12). Mix with the salt, vinegars, mustard, and pepper and let sit for 5 minutes to marinate and temper the shallot. Stir in the olive oil with a fork or a whisk: if it thickens and emulsifies, fine; if not, also fine—just stir before using.

Dress spicy greens such as **arugula, watercress, frisée,** or **radicchio** with shallot and sherry vinaigrette.

Add a teaspoon of **paprika** and a ¼ teaspoon smoked paprika (pimentón de la Vera) and toss with warm chickpeas or spoon over peeled and sliced oranges and you'll go all the way to Seville!

Stay right here at home and cook a slice or two of **bacon**. Add some of the rendered fat to the vinaigrette, dress the greens, and crumble the bacon into the salad. Eggs, historically good with bacon, can be hard boiled (page 30) and chopped on top. Or, instead of greens, dress sliced, boiled potatoes or boiled green beans (page 171) like this.

CREAMY MUSTARD DRESSING

Made creamy with an egg yolk, this dressing goes especially well spooned over cooked and cooled beets or boiled and cooled asparagus, green beans, or cauliflower. It's also a classic dressing for coleslaw.

1 egg yolk	½ teaspoon salt
1 or 2 teaspoons Dijon mustard	Freshly ground black pepper
1 teaspoon red wine vinegar	½ cup olive oil
1 teaspoon lemon juice	

A whole egg yolk is actually too much, so scoop half of it out (or just double the recipe). Whisk the mustard, vinegar, lemon juice, salt, and pepper together with the remaining yolk. Whisk in the oil slowly to create a creamy emulsion, like mayonnaise: stir quickly, dripping in the oil until the yolk and mustard begin to hold it and thicken, about a third of the way through. Now you can pour the oil in a little quicker, in a stream, but don't stop stirring. Keep going, and at about the two-thirds mark, it tends to get a little thick, so add a teaspoon of water and then whisk in the rest of the oil. Taste. More lemon?

If the dressing breaks and looks curdled, you can do one of two things:

> Nothing—because it doesn't really have to be emulsified, especially if you are using it to dress coleslaw or lettuces where the consistency of the dressing won't really matter.

> Something—fix it. See Mayonnaise (page 248).

For extra sweet-creaminess, add a couple tablespoons of cream. Or sour cream, buttermilk, crème fraîche, or yogurt.

To make **coleslaw**, cut a head of red or green cabbage into quarters and slice each across as thinly as you can. Toss the shredded cabbage with salt and a sprinkle of vinegar or lemon juice and set aside for 10 minutes to wilt slightly. Meanwhile, thinly slice some red onion and in a separate little bowl, sprinkle with salt and vinegar or lemon juice and set aside to marinate. Peel and grate a couple of carrots and toss with the cabbage. Spoon on the mustard dressing, grind in some black pepper, add the onion, and mix well. Taste and correct for salt, acid, and mustard. Let coleslaw sit for 30 minutes or up to 1 or 2 days and it only gets better.

AVOCADO AND HERB DRESSING

We also call it green goddess, especially in Berkeley, where the avocados and the locals are very green, and the goddess blesses from stickers on every other bumper.

---

4 tablespoons chopped herbs, (any combination of basil, mint, parsley, cilantro, tarragon, chives, chervil)

1 small garlic clove, pounded

½ avocado, pitted

1 teaspoon lemon or lime juice

½ teaspoon red wine vinegar

¼ teaspoon salt

Freshly ground black pepper

4 tablespoons olive oil

Pound the herbs in a mortar with the garlic, or just chop them extra fine and put in a small bowl with the garlic. Mash in the avocado and add the citrus juice, vinegar, salt, and pepper. Using the pestle or a whisk, add the olive oil in a thin stream to make a thick emulsion. Taste, correct, and use to dress romaine or butter lettuces.

Wedges of roasted beets, dressed with oil and vinegar, are colorful and delicious around a lettuce salad with avocado and herb dressing. Or you can skip the lettuces and just spoon the dressing over **sliced cucumbers**, **beets**, **and the other half of the avocado.**

A bowl of green goddess is welcome as a **sauce** at a **fried fish dinner** or with **fried vegetables**. Also spooned over **grilled chicken**, **boiled potatoes**, or a plate of **Hard-Boiled Eggs** (page 30).

Use also as a splendid **sandwich dressing** or for when leftovers like last night's **roasted chicken** (Chapter 9), say, or **pork tacos** (page 225) on July 5, are in need of a little sauce.

CITRUS ZEST VINAIGRETTE

The California winter brings a sweet confusion of citrus fruits, and every year it seems there are new varieties at the markets. This vinaigrette can use up a little of all of those grapefruit, kumquat, clementine, Meyer lemon, and tangerine rinds if you have them, but it is also remarkably good with just lemon and orange zests. It's perfect poured over a platter of sliced avocados with peeled and sliced oranges or roasted beets (page 183).

1 teaspoon zest: lemon, orange, lime, grapefruit . . .	1½ teaspoons red wine vinegar
1 tablespoon small-diced shallot	¼ teaspoon salt
2 teaspoons lemon or orange juice	Freshly ground black pepper
	3 tablespoons olive oil

The citrus zest has to be in very tiny pieces for this dressing, and there are a couple of ways to accomplish this. One is to use a vegetable peeler to cut strips of skin from the fruit, line up the strips and cut them into little sticks, and then line up the sticks and cut them into tiny bits. Another is to use the smallest holes on the box grater and then go over the gratings with a knife. Or, if you must, use a Microplane (which, for me, creates too feathery an effect—I like little bits, not microbits). Mix the shallot, citrus juice, vinegar, salt, and pepper with the zest and let sit for 5 minutes to marinate the shallot. Stir in the oil.

Toss **boiled vegetables** (page 171) with this bright dressing or spoon it on **grilled or baked fish fillets**.

Add ½ teaspoon minced or grated **fresh ginger** and ½ teaspoon toasted, crushed **coriander seeds** to the shallots. Use as above and for sliced **cucumber and zucchini salad**.

BUNKHOUSE DRESSING

What if you find yourself with ancient olive oil or no olive oil? What if the vinegar is the distilled sort best saved for washing windows? Only have bright yellow squeeze-bottle mustard? When what was in the house was unusable bunk, we came up with bunkhouse: a tasty dressing that didn't rely on our usual staples. At first, we made it only when we were on vacation, unprepared and far from the comforts of our home pantry. Necessity has mothered inflection and now we modify it to dress cucumbers, iceberg and romaine, boiled green beans, cauliflower, and more, at home or away. Be sure to use plain yogurt, and though canola or other vegetable oils work just fine, if you do have good olive oil, by all means use that.

1 garlic clove, pounded	3 tablespoons plain whole-milk yogurt
¼ teaspoon salt	
Juice of ½ lemon or lime (about 1½ tablespoons)	2 tablespoons vegetable oil or olive oil

Mix the garlic, salt, lemon juice, and yogurt together in a small bowl. Add the oil in slowly, stirring all the while to mix it well and keep the dressing from breaking—if it starts to separate, stir faster and pour slower.

Fresh **herbs** such as basil, mint, or cilantro really spruce up the bunkhouse. The simplest way to use them is to just pick whole leaves off the stems and toss them in with the salad. You can also chop and pound them up with the garlic and mix into the dressing.

In India, this is **raita**, the ubiquitous sauce that tastes so good on so many dishes. Oil is not always part of it, but the main difference is how it is used: scooped up with bread, spooned over spicy chickpeas, dolloped alongside sliced meats or tomatoes. Raita can be as simple as plain yogurt

with garlic, or it can include whole toasted seeds such as cumin or mustard, grated cucumbers or carrots, chopped tomatoes, and chopped herbs such as parsley, mint, and cilantro.

Bunkhouse dressing becomes **bunkHouse of Curry dressing** by replacing the lemon with lime and adding curry powder (or any combination of ground cumin, coriander, clove, fennel, black pepper, paprika, cayenne, and turmeric—the turmeric gives curry its distinctive color so is best not left out) and grated ginger if you like. This dressing is surely more British Raj than authentic Indian subcontinent, but *my* first encounter with something like it was in New Jersey where I was waiting tables at a steakhouse, and it was, for no good reason, the house dressing.

5

PASTA WITH TOMATO

Growing up, we ate pasta only one way. In fact, my mother never referred to it as pasta at all. It was called spaghetti, it had tomato sauce, ground beef, and an "Italian seasoning" packet, and I loved it. I've had pasta many ways since then, of course, but my family and I still love pasta best, or at least better, with tomatoey sauces. These recipes make enough sauce to dress 1 pound of pasta. The shapes suggested are those that I like to match with the particular sauce but really are interchangeable. A few other things to know:

- The tomatoes used in this chapter are canned whole, peeled tomatoes. Lift them from the can with a fork and tear them open so that the juice runs back into the can. It's not that you don't want the juice, just that it's better to cook the chopped tomato drier at first, so it gets kind of fried in the oil. Then, as your sauce needs liquid, you can tip some of the tomato juice into the pan. This slow frying in olive oil is an important part of making good tomato sauce with a luscious texture.

If it's tomato season and you have some ripe ones you'd rather cook with instead, there are several ways to proceed. Simplest is to grate the tomato on the biggest holes of a box-type cheese grater: cut the tomatoes in half at their equators and gently squeeze to get the seeds out, and then grate on the cut side into a bowl. Grate right down until all you have left is the skin—it won't go through the holes, so you can really push it onto the grater. Cook this pulpy tomato mash as you would chopped canned tomatoes. A bit more involved method, and good for when you find yourself with an abundance of ripe tomatoes, is roasting and milling (page 184). Fancier still is to make tomato concassé: Slip the tomatoes into your pasta pot of boiling water. Fish them out when the skins feel loose, around 30 seconds, and drop them in a bowl of ice water or just rinse in cold tap water. With a paring knife, cut out the green stem end and pull off the skin. If it's very stuck, drop the tomato back in the pot for a few seconds more. Cut the tomatoes in half at their equators and gently squeeze, cut side facing down, to get the seeds out. Cut the halves into dice. Use concassé just as you would chopped canned tomatoes, but cook them less so that their fresh texture and flavor are retained. All three of these fresh tomato methods have the same aim: to get rid of the skins and seeds. If you are happy to eat the skins and seeds, then just core, slice, and dice your ripe tomato as is.

• Grated cheese should be grated by you or someone you know. Our flush favorites are Parmigiano-Reggiano and Pecorino Toscano. When we're frugal, it's Grana Padano, and Pecorino Romano for when we're feeling a little salty.

• Most of these recipes call for ¼ cup of olive oil. If this seems like a lot, remember that in a sense, olive oil *is* the sauce. Olive oil unites

the ingredients and, with a splash from the pasta pot, shepherds them to sauce-hood.

• A good number of sauces call for crushed red pepper flakes. I find the spiciness of crushed red pepper flakes can vary greatly, so I recommend starting conservatively with a pinch of about ⅛ teaspoon. Taste the sauce once the crushed red pepper flakes have kindled it, and add more to fan the flames if you like.

• Many pasta sauces and indeed many dishes in general benefit from some chopped parsley and other fresh herbs. Herbs do something great to pasta sauces, making you aware of the color green in ways other than visual. I'm including parsley in a lot of these recipes, but you should cook them anyway if you don't have any. If you do, chop a loose ½ cup of picked leaves to yield the 2 tablespoons called for. See Salsa Verde (page 244) for more about preparing parsley and other herbs.

• Before you throw in the pasta, add plenty of salt to the rapidly boiling water. The reason to add salt to pasta water is, despite what you may have heard, really very simple: the pasta gets seasoned in the salty water and it tastes better. It's not to raise the temperature of the water or anything to do with preventing stickage; that can be easily prevented by plenty of water in a large pot and stirring several times during the cooking, especially at the beginning. For my 2-gallon pasta pot, I add 2½ tablespoons of salt, but the way to know how much you want to add is to get a spoon and taste the water: keep adding until you can taste the salt, in a pleasant way. Don't worry if it seems like a lot—it won't all get into the pasta; most of it stays with the water and goes down the drain. Olive oil added to the water is unnecessary: it just floats on top, then goes the way of the water. Keep at a fast boil the whole time and don't cover the pot. Stir irregularly, and when the pasta is done the way you like it—again, the only way to know is to pull out a piece and taste it—save a cup of the water in case you need it to thin the sauce, and then drain the pasta in a colander. I often just serve the pasta 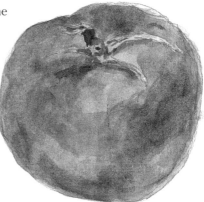 in the skillet the sauce was cooked in, but if I'm using a platter or bowl, I warm it up first with a ladleful of the pasta water.

• Remember: the sauce can wait for the pasta, but not the other way around.

• Though you'll be making these sauces in a pan, you don't want a deep saucepan for pasta sauces. You need a flat skillet that will hold not only the sauce, but all the pasta as well since they get mixed in the pan before serving. I like a heavy-bottomed All-Clad sauté pan or a cast-iron skillet, but whatever you have will work. Faced with the double whammy of a sluggish electric stove and a thin cheap pan when I really need to get dinner cooking, I turn on all four burners to different settings and move the pan around to regulate the heat. Not very energy efficient, but I try to move quickly in the kitchen to make up for it.

• The final step is a very important one: tasting and correcting the flavor, and particularly the texture, which is key to making really great plates of pasta instead of noodles that just happened to arrive at the table sharing space with the sauce. Once you've drained the pasta (saving some of the water) and mixed it with the sauce in the pan, twirl in a fork and take a bite. Think about saltiness and spiciness, also acidity, but don't forget to notice the consistency of the sauce and how it clings to the pasta. Move some of the pasta aside and look at the bottom of the pan. There should be a little liquid there, a little juiciness. The olive oil and the starchy pasta water will combine to give the sauce a shiny, slightly thickened quality that sticks to the pasta. If yours looks too watery, turn up the heat and stir it around for a minute to evaporate some of the liquid. If too dry, add a splash of the pasta water and stir well. A last shot of olive oil is very often in order.

marinara

"Tomato sauce, Dad. Not spicy, not bacony. Not fishy! Just plain. Can't we have that?" Liam asks with all the uncomplicated wisdom of the seven-year-old that he is.

"Yes, honey, we can," I reply, able to recognize sage advice when I hear it.

And we often do make a plain and satisfying sauce from just onions, a little garlic, and a can of tomatoes. I will give you that recipe and it's very good indeed, and great with meatballs, but let me just first say that if it is summer, and maybe you grew some tomatoes, or a friend did, or you found some irresistible and ripe at the market, there is also a fresh marinara that can be profoundly good, like the summer sun itself came down, put on an apron, and made you lunch. Okay, I'll give you that recipe, too.

SUMMER MARINARA

2 or 3 large ripe tomatoes

Salt

4 tablespoons olive oil

2 garlic cloves, very thinly sliced

1 bunch basil, leaves only, very
roughly chopped (about
1 packed cup)

1 scant cup ricotta (if you can
possibly find it, sheep's-milk is the
best), optional

1 pound rigatoni or fettuccine

Parmesan cheese

Put a big pot of cold water on to boil. Add salt.

If you don't mind tomato skins and seeds, or if you're in a hurry, just
cut the tomatoes into large dice about the size of, well, dice. If you
prefer to skin and seed the tomatoes, make tomato concassé (page
98). To draw out some liquid and intensify the flavor, put the diced
tomatoes in a colander, sprinkle with ½ teaspoon salt, and let sit for
10 minutes or, if you're still in a hurry, don't.

Put the pasta in the pot of boiling, salted water. Stir frequently. This
is a quick sauce and will be done before the pasta is, but you can also
wait to boil the pasta until the sauce is done.

Heat a large skillet to low and add the oil, then the garlic. Stir a bit
and add the basil and a sprinkle of salt. Raise the heat and cook the
basil, stirring, until it's wilted and dark green, watching that you
don't burn the garlic. Add the tomatoes, sprinkle with the salt (if you
haven't already), and cook until they just lose their rawness, about
5 minutes. If the pasta isn't cooked yet—taste a piece to see—turn
off the sauce until right before you drain the pasta, and then bring it

back up to speed. When the pasta is done, drain it and toss it in the pan with the sauce, tasting and making the proper adjustments. Toss in the ricotta, if using, but don't mix it in all the way; leave some streaks and lumps. Pass the Parmesan to grate.

Summer marinara can be nicely made with halved **cherry tomatoes** as well—just cook them a little less.

Pasta with summer marinara sauce becomes the Sicilian classic **pasta alla Norma** with the addition of roasted cubes of eggplant, chopped mint, and ricotta salata instead of fresh ricotta. Heat the oven to 425°F and peel stripes from the eggplant: it's nice to have some, but not all, of the skin. Cut the eggplant into 1-inch cubes, toss with oil and salt, and roast on a baking sheet until browned and very tender, about 20 minutes. When you can easily squish a cube with your finger, the eggplant will have a nice creamy texture; undercooked eggplant can have a less appealing, cottony feel. Follow the recipe for summer marinara, adding some crushed red pepper flakes with the garlic. Add the roasted eggplant when the tomatoes are cooked and let the sauce simmer gently until the pasta is ready. Toss in chopped mint and parsley and replace the fresh ricotta with crumbled or coarsely grated ricotta salata.

When asked why it is called alla Norma, be ready with your own story or use this one: it was named after Sicilian composer Vincenzo Bellini's opera of the same name because it was thought to be just as perfectly delicious.

NOT-SUMMER MARINARA

Salt

4 tablespoons olive oil

1 yellow onion, diced

2 garlic cloves, finely chopped

Crushed red pepper flakes (about ⅛ teaspoon)

1 15-ounce can whole peeled tomatoes, chopped, juice reserved

1 pound rigatoni or fettuccine

1 tablespoon chopped parsley

Put a big pot of cold water on to boil. Add salt.

Heat a large skillet over medium-low heat and add the oil, then the onion and a light sprinkle of salt. Cook the onion until soft and lightly browned. Add the garlic and red pepper flakes, cook a minute more, and add the chopped tomatoes and a little more salt. Raise the heat and bring the sauce to a simmer while you boil the pasta, stirring frequently. As the skillet gets to looking (and sounding) dry and sizzly, add doses of the reserved tomato juice.

When the pasta is done, drain it and toss it in the pan with the sauce, tasting and making the proper adjustments. Water, any remaining tomato juice, oil, salt? Parsley? Parsley!

Use butter to cook the onions, extra red pepper flakes, and ¼ cup of cream added to bubble for a minute in the finished sauce and this is **pasta alla vodka**, which I have always thought much better without the confounding vodka. If you feel bound by tradition to add it, sprinkle the vodka over the pasta in the pan—with great restraint, please, like vermouth in a dry martini, which is perhaps where the vodka would be better employed, though even there I prefer gin. A pink pasta sauce, which gets pinker as you add more cream.

Not-summer marinara can become **pasta alla Claudia,** a dish taught to me by the frugal girlfriend of a prickly communist graduate student I met in Florence many years ago. Omit the garlic and instead sizzle some chopped capers and lemon zest in with the cooked onions. Skip the red pepper flakes but not the parsley.

ARRABBIATA

Though the term is often translated as "angry," I prefer "enraged" to describe the spicy mood of this simple sauce. I first ate a plate of it in an outdoor summer-only restaurant along a river outside of Lucca. It was one of only two pastas offered before the three main courses of steak, chicken, or trout, all grilled. The trout were pulled from a small pond formed by the dammed river and carried past the table still flopping in a net, and while they (and the fried potatoes and mixed salad that were the only sides available with the grilled meats) were delicious, it was the spaghetti arrabbiata at Ristorante Purgatorio that got to me and instantly became my standard. But there was something giving it that distinction that I couldn't quite identify. I suspected that it was a bit of anchovy in the sauce, a suspicion supported by the fact that they absolutely forbade us to put Parmesan on this pasta (there are food rules in Italy that are taken very seriously, and not mixing fish and cheese is one of them). The chef vigorously denied that there was any anchovy, just olive oil, garlic, hot pepper, and tomato in his arrabbiata. After many attempts to make it as good myself, I finally hit upon the secret: a very slow cooking of the garlic and hot pepper. Simple, in the way that Tuscan food will be, and though I never got confirmation that that was how they did it at Purgatorio, it's how I've cooked it ever since. At our house we don't, but you can boldly flout the rules and grate on Parmesan if you like, reveling in your subversion.

Salt

4 tablespoons olive oil

2 garlic cloves, finely chopped

Enough crushed red pepper flakes to enrage but not engulf

2 tablespoons chopped parsley

1 15-ounce can whole peeled tomatoes, chopped, juice reserved separately

1 pound spaghetti

Put a big pot of cold water on to boil. Add salt.

Put the oil in a large skillet and begin to heat slowly. Add the garlic and red pepper flakes and adjust the heat so that the garlic just barely moves, cooking very slowly in the oil. This takes some attention, so don't walk away, and be sure to have your tomatoes ready. You and everyone in the house should smell the garlic, but it shouldn't even sizzle—if you can hear it, turn it down. The garlic should just sort of slowly wiggle, turning opaque and fragrant in the warming oil. Stir the garlic, and after about 3 minutes, before any hint of browning appears, add the chopped parsley. Stir for 20 seconds and then add the tomatoes. Raise the heat and bring the sauce to a simmer while you cook the pasta in the salted, boiling water. Stir frequently. As the skillet gets to looking (and sounding) dry and sizzly, add doses of the reserved tomato juice. Taste the pasta, and when it is done, drain it and toss it in the pan with the sauce, tasting and making the proper adjustments.

Simpler still is **aglio e olio,** the ultimate pantry pasta. Proceed with the cooking of the garlic and crushed red pepper flakes, but bypass the tomato. Just add the cooked pasta, a splash of the pasta water, and some chopped parsley if you have it. It can be enormously satisfying just like that and, with a green salad, makes a nice supper or lunch.

AMATRICIANA

This is the pasta that has become a family fallback, and though sometimes overexposed, it's still the favorite at our house. It is popular not only for its ability to satisfy and comfort but also because it, like puttanesca and arrabbiata, can be made from ingredients that are among the staples in our pantry. It's probably the one that my sons are most accomplished at making; in fact, personal preference variations have emerged in the making of amatriciana in our kitchen: some like to sauté onions to start the sauce, whereas others find that all the sweetness needed is handled by the bacon and tomato. Maybe try it both ways and decide for yourself.

Salt

2 tablespoons olive oil

¼ pound sliced bacon, cut across into short sticks, or pancetta or, most authentically, guanciale, which is pork cheek cured like pancetta

2 garlic cloves

Crushed red pepper flakes

1 15-ounce can peeled whole tomatoes, chopped, juice reserved separately

1 pound bucatini or spaghetti

2 tablespoons chopped parsley

Pecorino Romano or Parmesan cheese

Put a big pot of cold water on to boil. Add salt.

Heat a large skillet over medium heat and add 1 tablespoon of the oil and the bacon. Cook until the bacon starts to brown around the edges, less than 5 minutes. If there's too much fat in the pan, take a little out, but save it. Add the garlic and red pepper flakes, cook for just a moment, and add the tomatoes. Raise the heat and bring the sauce to a simmer while you boil the pasta, stirring it frequently. As the skillet gets to looking (and sounding) too dry and sizzly, add doses of the reserved tomato juice. When the pasta is done, drain it and toss it in the pan with the sauce and parsley, tasting and making the proper adjustments (think: oil, bacon fat, pasta water, salt, spiciness). Pass the cheese to grate.

Amatriciana and other simple pastas are often the meals we eat when we get home late and are hungry or just haven't really planned anything for dinner. To make these pastas a bit more substantial, sometimes I'll drop (carefully) **an egg per person** in the boiling water a minute or two after I put in the pasta. When it's done, so will the egg be hard boiled and ready to peel, cut, salt, and eat atop the pasta. Hunger, get thee behind me!

Another Roman masterpiece of simplicity is **pasta alla gricia**: the sauce is Amatriciana without the tomato. The coming together of the pork fat and the pasta water is what makes it happen here.

PUTTANESCA

The name of this sauce has been around the block, and it's a well-walked block. Even without the provocative name, pasta puttanesca is perfect for a late-night *spaghettata*—a meal of pasta eaten at an unusual hour (part of what I love about Italy is that they have a word for something like that!). *Spaghettata* also means "beautiful mess," a definition that fits puttanesca *perfettamente*. Individually, capers, olives, and anchovies each pack a concentration of flavor; it's the combining of the three that gives puttanesca its salty, spicy, and ribald character. Blasphemous, maybe (another Italian rule holds that a dish may include onions or garlic, not both), but I make puttanesca with well-cooked red onions: their mild sweetness plays nice with Team Caper-Olive-Anchovy.

Salt

4 tablespoons olive oil

1 medium red onion, thinly sliced

6 anchovy fillets, chopped

2 garlic cloves, finely chopped

Crushed red pepper flakes

1 15-ounce can peeled whole tomatoes, chopped, and juice reserved separately

2 tablespoons capers, well soaked and drained, if salt packed, and roughly chopped

¼ cup pitted and roughly chopped Niçoise or other black olives

1 pound penne or spaghetti

2 tablespoons chopped parsley

1 teaspoon chopped oregano or marjoram

Put a big pot of cold water on to boil. Add salt.

Heat a large skillet on high heat and add the oil, then the onion and a light sprinkle of salt. Stir the onion until it gets going and then lower the heat to medium and cook, stirring occasionally, until soft and well browned, about 20 minutes. It should taste very savory-sweet. Add the anchovies and cook for a minute or two so that they melt into the onion, then add the garlic and red pepper flakes, stirring and smelling the good, not burning, garlic. Add the tomatoes, capers, and olives. Raise the heat and bring the sauce to a simmer while you boil the pasta. As the skillet gets to looking (and sounding) dry and sizzly, add doses of the reserved tomato juice. When the pasta is done, drain it and toss it in the pan with the sauce, parsley, and oregano, tasting and making the proper adjustments.

RAGÙ FINTO (MEAT SAUCE, QUICK-STYLE)

Most pasta sauces can be made in the time it takes for a big pot of cold water to come to a boil. Some take much longer, and in learning to know the difference, there may be some moments of disappointment and of hunger (or at least satisfaction delayed). It became clear that my son Henderson hadn't completed this part of his cooking education one night as I was tasting the evening's dishes at Chez Panisse. Saturday night at five o'clock is a crunchy moment at the restaurant. Late lunchers are trying not to look toward the door, knowing they must leave soon to make room for the dinner crowd but still lingering in Zinfandel afterglow. Early diners are waiting at the bar, and everywhere bussers and waiters are working hard to clean up after the 200 people who just had lunch while getting ready for the 250 coming in for dinner. The cooks are setting up their stations and, though tensed for the headlong rush about to begin, seem calm: the open kitchen can't hide chaos on either side, so we try mightily to keep a sane appearance. This is also "tasters" time (we taste one of everything on the menu every day— the number one secret to good cooking in a restaurant and at home: taste always), and I am at the salad station in the midst of trying one of the first courses when the sauté cook leans over to say that Henderson is on the phone from New York. We are a close crew and they know my sons well. They also can't help but overhear, so the culinary comedy of the conversation that follows is lost on no one.

"Hey, Dad. Sorry, I know you're busy, but I'm making Bolognese and can I just ask you a quick question? Don't hang up."

"Sure." I wasn't going to.

"Okay. What's the best meat to use?"

"Well, what kind have you got?"

"I'm going to the store now."

"But Bolognese takes hours to cook, and in New York it's, what, eight o'clock now? Is the store even open? Oh, sorry, it's New York, right." I roll my eyes at the cooks and squeeze a little lemon on the rocket salad we are trying. The faces of cooks and waiters around me show a mix of amusement at the content of our conversation and amazement that it's even taking place just as the curtain is going up on the evening.

"I can get the meat, just what kind?"

"Even if you get it now, you won't start cooking till nine, won't be done till like midnight." Oh, sorry, it's New York. Right.

"Yeah, but I'm on my way, walking to the store now."

"I think you should get some eggs and whatever salad looks okay, bread, cheese maybe. Bolognese is going to have to be for another night. Can I call you back later?"

I called him later and he did have eggs and good toast for dinner that night, but it made me think about getting a Bolognese-like sauce recipe to him. Something you could make up pretty quickly but that would satisfy like that classic long-cooked meat sauce from Bologna. Pork should be the meat in it because, as my friend's mother says, "Pork just tastes better." Or, as my other friend says, "Chicken has become the default cheap meat, but it really ought to be pork. Pork already is what we think chicken should be. Pork is more chicken than chicken." She's probably right, but what I love about ground pork for a pasta sauce is its sweet, rich flavor and its ability to quickly cook to tenderness. The sauce I came up with can, in fact, cook in the 30 or so minutes it takes to boil the water and cook the pasta, but it's a bit better if there's time to simmer longer.

Salt

1 pound ground pork or pork sausages, taken out of the skins

2 tablespoons olive oil

Freshly ground black pepper

Crushed red pepper flakes

¾ teaspoon each toasted and ground fennel and coriander seeds (optional)

1 yellow onion, sliced

2 tablespoons chopped parsley

2 garlic cloves, chopped finely

1 15-ounce can peeled whole tomatoes, chopped, juice reserved separately

1 pound rigatoni or penne

Parmesan cheese

Put a big pot of cold water on to boil. Add salt.

Spread out the ground pork like a hilly landscape on the paper it was wrapped in, or on a plate, sprinkle with ½ teaspoon salt, and grind on some black pepper. If desired, for a more sausage-y effect, sprinkle with red pepper flakes and toasted and ground fennel and coriander seeds.

Spreading the meat out like this shows more surface area to the seasonings and requires less handling to mix it in. Overhandling ground meat can make it turn tough, so don't. Fold up the patty of pork and mix it just until the spices are well distributed. Of course, if you're using sausage, then skip these seasoning steps.

Heat a large skillet over medium-high heat. Add 1 tablespoon of the oil and then quickly add the pork, breaking it into chunks and placing it in the hot pan bit by bit. Tilt the pan to spread the oil around and nudge the pork around to fill in the gaps and get even browning, but don't move it around too much. The skillet should be at full-throated sizzle—if it's too quiet, turn up the heat. Resist the temptation to poke and stir at this point; just let the meat fry: it will go from pink to gray and, if you stay out of its way, to a nice caramel brown, which looks and tastes much better, sweeter. When the first side is ready, turn the pieces over and brown the other side. Set the pork aside on a plate and tip out some of the grease if it makes you feel better, though I generally find myself adding it back in later.

Add the remaining tablespoon of oil, if needed, and the onion. Sprinkle with salt and stir with a wooden spoon to scrape up the bits of browned meat as the onion begins to get juicy. Lower the heat to medium and cook the onion, stirring occasionally, until very tender, about 15 minutes. Add the parsley, garlic, and red pepper flakes and stir for a minute as the garlic sizzles, but don't let it get even a little bit browned. When the garlic smells really good, add the tomatoes and the pork. Use the back of the spoon on any chunks that are too big, and adjust the heat so that the sauce is simmering but not bubbling fast. At this point, you can cook the pasta in the salted, boiling water, stirring frequently, and the sauce will be done in the 10 or so minutes it takes to cook, though it will get better if given another 10 for the pork and tomatoes to enjoin.

If the pan starts to dry out and sizzle, add some of the juice from the tomatoes or, if you've used all the juice, a little water. Chicken (page 206) or pork (page 222) stock works very well also, but water is fine.

Taste the pasta, and when it is done, drain and add it to the sauce, and toss, stir, and toss. Taste it; you may want to add some salt, oil, or the pork fat you set aside—or a splash of the pasta water if it needs more flow. Serve hot and pass the cheese to grate.

When I was fourteen, I had a girlfriend who was way ahead of me. She had older brothers who loved extreme skiing movies and the Rolling Stones, and I remember how they laughed at me when I declared the Stones' cover of "Jumpin' Jack Flash" inferior to Peter Frampton's original. I still blush like an adolescent boy when I think of my folly (she broke up with me a month later), but sometimes it's like that: you get to liking the imitation so well that you start seeing it as the real thing. I didn't know that pistachios weren't red, that "butter" was margarine, that tomato soup wasn't born in a can, and Warhol didn't design the label. Enlightened, if humiliated, I am delighted with the originals—Mick inarguably does "Jumpin' Jack Flash" better than Peter, but wouldn't it be cool if it turned out that Andy started as some guy in the Campbell's design department?

When I have the time to make the original ragù, **Bolognese**, I dice the onion along with carrots and celery and replace half of the pork with beef. I use chicken stock (page 206) to give it richness and an especially luxurious texture. The sauce can be started and finished on the stovetop or finished in the oven. If you choose to keep the pan on the burner, turn it very low so that the sauce bubbles contentedly. Add stock or water in doses, every 15 minutes or so, as the liquid in the pan reduces. When the pork is quite tender and begins to get very comfortable in its velvety-textured surroundings, it's done, usually a couple hours. For a richer, but somehow not heavier, effect, use whole milk for your last addition of liquid. To cook the ragù in a 325°F oven, add enough liquid to the pan so that the meat is covered by a quarter inch or so, bring to a simmer, and slide into the oven. Check every half hour, adding more liquid if needed. Chef Boyardee wishes he made it like this.

Ragù finto is also good with greens replacing the tomato: coarsely chop and wash some kale or chard and boil it tender in the pasta pot before you cook the pasta. Scoop it out, drain it, and add the cooked greens to the sausage and onion mixture.

My kids love Thai-restaurant food—maybe because it tends toward a sweetness that I often find a spoonful too much—but one dish we agree on is **larb**, the pungent, salty-sour salad of ground pork or beef. One night, mid–ragù finto making, I suddenly turned Thai-ward, inspired, for some reason, to leave the pasta for another time. When the pork was nearly done, I added sliced red onions to the skillet, along with finely chopped ginger and garlic. Shaking the skillet, I cooked in some rough-chopped cilantro and, after 30 seconds or so, splashed in some water, squeezed in a lemon, and added a judicious jolt of fish sauce. That time I didn't have jalapeños to chop and add, but next time I did. Serve it warm or at room temperature spooned over plain rice, sliced raw cabbage, or lettuce leaves.

SPAGHETTI AND MEATBALLS

Meat loaf and her plump little progeny, meatballs, are made from the same recipe. Myself, I am more baller than loafer, though the loaf, with its cloak of ketchup and side of mash, legitimately holds nostalgic appeal for many. Strategic advantages of meatballs include: versatility—any good-quality ground meat can be used; thrift—ground meats, even of the best quality, tend to be economical; and convenience—meatballs can be very successfully made ahead to cook later while also hitting high numbers on the leftover scale-of-usability once cooked. Additionally, meatballs can be outfitted with spices to travel the world from Mexico to Morocco, India, and Syria. This recipe is for the sort, immortalized in song, that sit atop spaghetti.

Salt

1 pound ground pork, beef, turkey, lamb, or chicken (a combination of meats can also be nice, especially if one of them is pork)

½ teaspoon freshly ground black pepper

2 slices stale bread or ½ cup dried bread crumbs

½ medium onion

1 garlic clove, pounded or very finely chopped

1 egg

2 tablespoons grated Parmesan or Pecorino cheese, plus more for serving

Crushed red pepper flakes

2 tablespoons chopped parsley

1 tablespoon chopped oregano or marjoram, or ½ teaspoon dried (optional but really good)

Light olive oil or vegetable oil, for pan-frying

½ cup chicken stock (page 206) or water

1 pound spaghetti

Put a big pot of cold water on to boil. Add salt.

Season the pork with ½ teaspoon salt and black pepper (see page 115). Tear the bread into small chunks and put them in a large bowl. With the large holes of a cheese grater, grate the onion onto the bread. Crack the egg into the bowl, and with your fingers, mush the onion, egg, and bread together. Set this mixture aside for 5 minutes so the bread can absorb the onion juice and the egg. Add a tablespoon or two of cold water or milk if your onion wasn't very juicy and the bread still seems dry. Add the cheese, red pepper flakes, parsley, oregano (if using), and seasoned meat to the bowl and mix thoroughly, squeezing the mixture through your hands until it's all of one consistency.

Heat a large skillet over medium heat. Make a small sample patty from the meatball mixture and fry it in a little oil on both sides until cooked through. Taste and correct, thinking about salt, herbs, cheese, and especially texture. Though I secretly want the test-meatball all to myself, I know that sharing with a helpful child shows generosity, a collaborative spirit, and a sense of familial engagement, so I reluctantly do. If both of you decide that the taster is too soft, try kneading the mixture for a minute to tighten it up. Too tough: soak some more bread in a little milk and gently work it in. Too dry: add some milk. Too wet: add some dried bread crumbs.

Using your hands, form about 20 Ping-Pong-ball-size meatballs. Refrigerate if not cooking soon. Reheat the skillet and add enough oil so that the pan shows no dry spots. Arrange the meatballs in the pan, starting at one side and filling to the other. Go back to where you started in the pan and turn the meatballs 2 or 3 times as they brown. Don't try to turn them too soon or they won't brown and may start to fall apart. (An easier way to cook the meatballs is simply to bake them on a baking sheet in a 450°F oven for 10 minutes. They don't quite brown up as much, but it's less work and less messy and very nearly as good.)

When well colored, tip off the excess oil if necessary and add the marinara sauce to the skillet. Stir gently to scrape up any browned bits and add a little stock or water if the sauce seems too thick. Boil the spaghetti while simmering the meatballs in the sauce to finish cooking through, about 10 minutes. Drain the pasta, add to the meatballs and marinara, toss, and taste. Pass the Parmesan . . . *all covered in cheese . . .*

If you don't have bread crumbs, ¾ cup boiled and **mashed potato** can be used instead and yields an especially tender, moist meatball.

Omit the grated cheese and oregano to make spicy international meatball variations:

- For **Mexican meatballs**, add cumin, cilantro, and green chilies to the mixture. Serve with Plain Rice (page 150) and boiled (page 171) or roasted (page 179) vegetables, or fold into tortillas with shredded cabbage, thinly sliced scallions, and a squeeze of lime juice.

- For **Moroccan meatballs**, replace some or all of the pork with ground lamb or beef and add cumin, garlic, mint, and ground dried red chili to the mixture. Use half the tomato amount for the sauce, and add cooked chickpeas (page 57) with their liquid, and garlicky Sautéed Greens (page 190). Serve with crusty bread or toasted pita.

- For **Indian meatballs**, replace some or all of the pork with ground lamb and add grated ginger, mint, and the C-spices: cumin, coriander, clove, cardamom, cinnamon, and cayenne. Use half the amount of tomato, add cooked chickpeas or lentils with their liquid, and serve with saffron rice (page 150) and a spoonful of yogurt or raita (page 94).

• For **Syrian meatballs**, replace some or all of the pork with ground lamb or beef and add paprika and the C-spices, replacing the cardamom with allspice. Shape the mixture into round or oval patties, thread on skewers if you like, and grill. Serve with Plain Rice (page 150) and a shredded carrot salad (page 40) or stuffed in a pita with sliced cucumbers and leaves of parsley, cilantro, mint, or dill. A topping of yogurt is good here, too.

Versatile meatballs can be flattened and grilled.

6

PASTA OTHERWISE

There are eleven reasons that we decide to make pasta otherwise. The first is that we're out of tomatoes. These delicious recipes are the other ten. Some, like carbonara, are quite rich, so we eat plates of them only occasionally and always with a green salad. Other times, while we're grilling meat or roasting a chicken and feeling a little Italian, we eat smaller bowlfuls, just enough to keep us wanting more.

See page 100 for general pasta cooking tips.

SAGE AND BUTTER

That you can make it when you can't find your olive oil isn't even the point. The point is that fettuccine with sage leaves sizzled in butter, grated over with cheese, and cracked with black pepper is going to become your winter favorite.

Salt	Parmesan cheese
1 pound fettuccine or spaghetti	Freshly ground black pepper
4 tablespoons (½ stick) butter	
½ bunch sage, leaves only, very roughly chopped (approximately ¼ cup)	

Put a big pot of cold water on to boil. Add salt. Boil the pasta, stirring frequently. Meanwhile, heat a skillet to medium. Add 3 tablespoons of the butter, and when it stops foaming, add the sage leaves and a sprinkle of salt. Stir and let the sage leaves sizzle until they turn a darker green, about 1 minute. Turn the heat to low and add a ladle of pasta water to stop them from getting too dark.

Taste the pasta and when it is done, drain it and add it to the pan with the remaining tablespoon of butter, stirring well and splashing in pasta water to give some flow. Taste, tweak, and serve with cheese to grate and pepper to grind.

If you want to eat less butter, you can make it with half **olive oil**. If you want to eat more butter, go for it.

In spring, cook some **peas** and add them to the pan. A little **cream** makes it a different dish but, added to the pan with the sage and butter and cooked a couple of minutes, can be very nice.

In winter, roast small cubes of **butternut squash** (page 154) or sliced **cauliflower** florets (page 179) and toss them into the skillet to laze in the butter a bit before adding the pasta. Or toss in boiled and chopped **kale**. Chopped toasted **hazelnuts** or **almonds**, too.

CARBONARA

This is the legendary pasta with the bacon and egg sauce that is creamy but, when properly made, without cream. The trick is in getting the egg yolks to mix with the pasta and a measure of the pasta water to thicken while staying fluid. It takes a little worthwhile practice. A jolt of black pepper counter-cracks the richness.

Salt	2 eggs
1 pound spaghetti	1 cup grated Parmesan cheese
2 tablespoons olive oil or butter	¼ teaspoon ground black pepper, or more to taste
¼ pound bacon or pancetta, cut into little strips	

Put a big pot of cold water on to boil. Add salt. Add the spaghetti when the water boils, stir frequently, and the sauce will be ready by the time it's done.

Warm a skillet over medium-low heat; add the oil and the bacon. Cook until the bacon starts to brown around the edges, less than 5 minutes. Splash in a little pasta water and turn the heat to very low while waiting for the pasta to cook.

In a small bowl, mix the eggs, cheese, ¼ teaspoon salt, and ¼ teaspoon pepper.

Taste a piece of pasta and just before it is done, reheat the skillet to low. Drain the pasta, save ½ cup of water, turn off the skillet, and add the pasta to the skillet, stirring to coat with the bacon fat. Add a little pasta water and then the egg mixture. Mix everything up together very well and add more pasta water if needed. Don't be afraid to add up to ¾ cup pasta water—the sauce will thicken as you eat and it cools, so make it a little looser than you otherwise might. Pass more cheese to grate and pepper to grind at the table.

Carbonara shouldn't really be messed with, but **peas** are nice in the spring.

Forget what should and shouldn't be and mess with carbonara: Make it with cream, and omit the bacon. You can call it **Alfredo** sauce if you like, or, in the spring asparagus season, make a version like a richer primavera that starts with sliced new onions or scallions and a little garlic (green, if available). Cook in olive oil or butter for a couple of minutes, then add asparagus, sliced on a bias so it's shaped like penne, and just enough water to halfway cover it. Add some salt, simmer, and when the asparagus is tender, most of the water should be gone. If not, tip it out so that just a little remains. Mix up 1 egg with 1 egg yolk and a cup of cream, ½ cup grated Parmesan, and black pepper. When the penne is done, drain it (save some water), add it into the skillet, turn off the heat, and stir in the cream mixture. Toss in chopped parsley and mint and stir well. Just as with carbonara, this sauce will thicken as it cools and the egg sets, so keep it loose with pasta water.

PRIMAVERA

In Italy they eat a dish of pasta with peas, cream, and prosciutto, but it's not called primavera and it's made strictly with peas: other vegetables would surely offend. Pasta primavera, with a variety of spring vegetables and its seasonal name, is really an American invention. The specifics of its origin are disputed, but there seems to be consensus that it came from the New York restaurant Le Cirque in the 1970s. The chef there, Jean Vergnes, was not only *not* the inventor of the dish, but thought it such an atrocity that, though it was much requested, he refused to allow it to be made in his kitchen. A pasta pot was set up in the hallway to meet the demand.

I feel no such outrage and happily cook it right in the kitchen, as should you, but I advise that you show some restraint: surely part of why Chef Jean didn't care for primavera was that cooks tend to throw every vegetable in there. Sticking to two or three kinds is a wiser choice. Try, for example: peas, asparagus, and scallions; spinach, carrots, and cauliflower; zucchini, cherry tomatoes, and lots of basil.

Salt

1 tablespoon olive or vegetable oil

2 tablespoons (¼ stick) butter

1 small onion, sliced

1 red bell pepper, stemmed, seeded, and thinly sliced

1 cup loosely packed basil or mint leaves, roughly chopped

Crushed red pepper flakes

1 cup cream

1 pound farfalle

½ pound green beans, stemmed and cut in 1-inch pieces

Parmesan cheese

Put a big pot of cold water on to boil. Add salt.

Heat a skillet over high heat and add the oil and butter, then the onion, bell pepper, and ½ teaspoon salt. Stir until the onion and pepper get going and then lower the heat to medium and cook, stirring occasionally, until soft, about 10 minutes. Add the basil and red pepper flakes and stir for a minute. Add the cream and ¼ cup water and bring to a low simmer. Add the pasta to the boiling water, stir frequently, and when it is 5 minutes from done, add the green beans and a pinch of salt to the skillet (you can also boil the green beans separately and stir them into the sauce right before the pasta). Drain the pasta and add it to the pan with a splash of its water if needed—the sauce will thicken as it cools, so make it a little looser than you otherwise might. Pass the Parmesan for grating at the table.

BIBO'S ZUCCHINI PASTA

My dear friend Bibo has always been one of my best supporters. She was especially helpful when I decided to make a career change from artist to cook, sending me to apply at the best restaurants she knew, giving me a place to stay and the opportunity to hone my beginner's skills in her rudimentary Berkeley kitchen. Together we threw big dinner parties with nothing more than a glorified hot plate, a Weber grill, and an electric convection oven that kept tripping the circuit breaker, throwing the gathered gleeful into even more gleeful darkness.

The one thing that Bibo did not support, however, was my decision to cook zucchini frittatas as a part of my tryout lunch for a job at Chez Panisse. Her disdain for zucchini was born of her upbringing in New England, where each summer yields what she is not alone in considering a gross overabundance of that soft squash, resulting in a nauseating bottomless buffet of it fried, pickled, stewed, and baked into breads. So when I told her that I planned to cook zucchini into little frittatas with fresh herbs and cheese for Alice and the other Chez Panisse chefs, she said no, you absolutely are not!

I respect Bibo's judgment and taste, so I considered her advice and then, modeling her healthy disregard for authority, ignored it and cooked them anyway. It turned out they were surprisingly delicious; they were right for the occasion, and they got me the job. I still sometimes make those little frittatas when the summer zucchini are in full force, as well as this simple, economical pasta, born out of those anxious days of experimentation.

Salt

4 small zucchini, a little under 1 pound

4 tablespoons olive oil, plus more as needed

1 pound penne

2 garlic cloves, chopped

Crushed red pepper flakes

2 tablespoons chopped mint

2 tablespoons chopped parsley

Butter, as needed

Parmesan or Pecorino cheese

Put a big pot of cold water on to boil. Add salt.

Wash the zucchini to get rid of any grit and cut off the ends. Do the roll cut: slice a triangle off the end of a zucchini, as if you're starting to make a point on it, but then roll it toward you a quarter turn and cut another wedge, your knife cutting diagonally across the face of the first cut. Keep rolling and cutting like this until you have a pile of angled shapes that are uneven but more or less the same size. (The roll cut also works very well for carrots that are to be roasted or boiled.)

Roll cut carrots just like zucchini.

Heat a skillet over high heat and then add the oil and, right away, the zucchini. Shake the pan to even things out and then leave it alone to brown, about 10 minutes. It should, as Liam offers, "sorta seem like it's burning." Turn the zucchini around to brown another side and leave it be for another few minutes. Sprinkle with 1 teaspoon salt and turn down the heat. Taste the zucchini: they should be sweet and caramelized, pretty soft, with no crunch.

Let the pan cool and cook the pasta in the salted boiling water. Stir frequently. Taste a piece, and a minute or two before it's done, warm the skillet and move the zucchini to the sides. Add a little more oil if needed, and put the garlic, red pepper flakes, and mint into the middle. Let it sizzle, and when the garlic is cooked, stir everything up and add a splash of water from the pot to keep the garlic from burning. Stir in the drained pasta and the parsley. Taste and see if maybe a glug more olive oil or a knob of butter isn't called for. Pass the Parmesan or Pecorino to grate.

BROCCOLI AND BACON

I have long suspected that parents who complain that their kids don't like vegetables actually don't like vegetables themselves. There may be other factors at play (see page 169 for some), but young kids will mostly do what their parents do: watch too much TV, not floss enough, and not eat their greens. Cooked in a skillet as for this pasta, and especially when cooked with bacon, broccoli has been a kid favorite in our house for always.

Salt	1 pound penne
2 tablespoons olive oil	2 garlic cloves, chopped
¼ pound sliced bacon, cut across into short sticks, or pancetta	Crushed red pepper flakes
	Crumb 2 (page 26), for optional sprinkling (about 1 cup)
1 broccoli head, florets and peeled main stalks sliced ¼ inch thick	Parmesan cheese

Put a big pot of cold water on to boil. Add salt.

Heat a skillet over medium and add 1 tablespoon of the olive oil and the bacon. Cook until the bacon starts to brown, less than 5 minutes, then set aside. Leaving the oil and fat in the skillet, raise the heat to high, put in the broccoli, and sprinkle with a scant ½ teaspoon salt. Stir to coat, then stop stirring for several minutes to let the broccoli brown. Stir/don't stir until the broccoli is browned and tender, about 7 minutes. Put the pasta in the pot and stir frequently. Turn the heat to low under the skillet, move the broccoli to the perimeter, and add the garlic and crushed red pepper center stage, adding oil if it's dry there. If the skillet is very hot, wait a minute so the garlic won't burn. Bring in the broccoli (*bring in the broccoli!*) when the garlic is just right and stir, adding a splash of pasta water. Stir in the bacon and drain the pasta and add to the skillet. Stir, toss, and taste. Top with oily crumbs and/or grated cheese.

BEANS AND GREENS

Spill more beans and a splash more liquid into this dish and it becomes the classic soup pasta fazool (page 61). Whether a soup or a pasta, as it is here, it's very good flavored with rosemary and sage, and sprinkled with oily bread crumbs.

Salt

4 tablespoons olive oil

1 medium red onion, diced

½ tablespoon whole rosemary or sage leaves, or both, coarsely chopped

1 garlic clove, chopped

Crushed red pepper flakes

½ pound spinach leaves, destemmed, washed, and drained

2 cups cooked white beans, with their liquid (1 scant cup dried)

1 pound penne or orecchiette

Parmesan cheese

Crumb 2 (page 26)

Strong herbs can be tamed by quickly frying until translucent.

Put a big pot of cold water on to boil. Add salt.

Heat a skillet over high heat and add the oil, then the onion and a light sprinkle of salt. Stir the onion until it gets going, then lower the heat to medium and cook, stirring occasionally, until soft and lightly browned, 15 to 20 minutes.

Add the rosemary and/or sage, stir, and cook for a minute. Add the garlic and red pepper flakes. When the garlic is fragrant but not browned at all, add the spinach. Stir and cook for a minute. If the spinach was dry going into the skillet, you may need to splash in a little of the bean water to keep the garlic from burning. Add the beans and a portion of their liquid, starting with ½ cup. Crush some of the beans with the back of a spoon to give the sauce thickness and cling. Boil the pasta, strirring frequently, as you simmer the sauce, adding more bean liquid or water if it gets dry. Drain the pasta, stir into the sauce, taste, correct, and serve. Pass cheese to grate and a bowl of oily crumbs to top.

Especially in summer, **tomatoes** are a nice addition. Chop them, add to the skillet after the garlic, and let cook for a few minutes before proceeding with the recipe.

Spinach can easily be replaced or supplemented by any number of greens—escarole leaves, roughly chopped and requiring a bit more cooking, are deservedly classic. If you are using heartier greens like **kale**, **chard**, or **beet greens**, boil them in the pasta water until tender, set aside, chop when cooled, and add in just as for the spinach.

PESTO

Maybe, like me, you've read pesto recipes that are so insistent on certain ingredients, tools, and techniques that after reading them you feel as if you can barely manage to pour yourself a glass of water with any authenticity, let alone achieve pesto sauce. This five-ingredient classic should be as easy to make as it is to love, and it is, especially if you have a blender. You don't need exactly the right tiny basil leaves from a Genovese hillside garden overlooking the sea, and you don't even need to have the mortar and pestle from which the sauce takes its name (through you ought to). You do need conviction, a generous bunch of fresh basil, decent olive oil, real Parmesan cheese, pine nuts, and garlic, and even if you don't have them all, there are substitutions for some of them. There is no substitute for conviction. To pair with pesto, spaghetti is best. Gemelli and trofie are also wonderful.

Scant ¼ teaspoon salt	½ teaspoon pounded garlic
1 big bunch basil, leaves only (about 3 lightly packed cups; see page 244 for more on preparing basil and other herbs)	½ cup grated Parmesan cheese, plus more for serving
	⅜ cup olive oil
Scant ¼ cup pine nuts, toasted tan, not brown (page 11)	1 pound spaghetti, gemelli, or trofie

Put a big pot of cold water on to boil. Add salt.

Push half of the basil leaves down into the blender. Add the pine nuts, garlic, salt, and cheese, top with the remaining basil leaves, and push it all down hard with a spoon. Add the oil and begin the pulse and push method. You don't want the blender to grind up only the leaves that are at the bottom, nor do you want it too finely pureed. The solution is to pulse the blender for a second, stir the contents with a spoon, and then tamp it all back down. Pulse again, push it down again. Repeat this process, taking care to remove the spoon before running the blender. (Seriously. I've ground the tip of a wooden spoon into pesto and it's not good. Splintery. So now I keep the button-pushing hand away while the spoon-wielding hand is at work.) Keep going, and shortly after everyone in your house is annoyed and begging you to stop, the pesto should be ground enough so that the blades catch and it all swirls around in a fragrant green conical whirl. You can hear it when it catches and all is being pureed, not just the stuff at the bottom. Though it *is* glorious, let it go for only a few seconds. The pesto should have flow but still be a little chunky. If it gets pale and creamy-looking, you've gone a little too far this time, but hey, the summer's just started. Taste and add what's needed and then pulse a final second to mix in any additions.

When the pesto is done, cook the pasta in the salted boiling water. Stir frequently. Put the pesto sauce into your serving bowl, and just before draining the pasta, stir a little of the water into the sauce to thin it slightly and make it easier to mix. Add the drained pasta, toss, taste, correct, and serve with cheese for grating.

When good basil is not available, you can replace it with 1 bunch **parsley** and a small handful of **marjoram** leaves, and trade the pine nuts for toasted walnuts. In winter, a quarter pound of **arugula** can also be substituted for the out-of-season basil. This Sicilian version is spicier, though, and needs the sweetness of ¼ cup each of pine nuts *and* walnuts, and ¼ cup more grated cheese to balance out its sharpness. Mint leaves can be added to arugula pesto or used in equal parts with parsley to make an aromatic pesto of their own for pasta sauce or a salsa for grilled lamb.

In summer, line plates

with sliced **tomatoes** and set tangles of pasta with pesto on top. In winter, slivered **sun-dried tomatoes** tossed in with the arugula version taste of longer, sunnier days.

There's a point in every basil season, late in the summer, when the pesto frustratingly turns brown when it contacts the hot pasta. If this bothers you, you can **boil half of the basil** very briefly in the pasta water to set the color. Scoop it out quickly and drop into a bowl of ice water. When cooled, squeeze handfuls of the boiled basil to get rid of as much water as you can, chop it up a bit, and add it to the blender with the raw basil.

Make a superior **potato salad** with lengths of boiled green beans and halved cherry tomatoes dressed, along with the boiled potatoes, with pesto.

MUSHROOMS

The winter rains in Northern California bring the wild mushrooms up, and bring us out into the woods after them. A committed forager since childhood (mostly of nonculinary bugs, frogs, and snakes), I learned as an adult how to identify in the woods the types of mushrooms I knew from the kitchen: fluted, orange chanterelles and squat, fat porcini. My porcini spot is rare enough to be guarded, so I bring along no interlopers when

Mushrooms are best quickly rinsed of grit and left to dry for a few minutes.

I go there. The chanterelles, on the other hand, are often abundant, so we will walk with family and friends, searching and picnicking beneath the oaks. In good years, mushrooms are easy to spot, especially from a child's low angle.

One February weekend, we headed for the foggy hills and brought along some friends of my sons', a brother and sister who lived across the street. They played at our house a lot—their single father working nights and weekends—and rarely got out of the city. At first they were cautious in the woods, unsettled by the lack of pavement, but they soon relaxed and ran with our kids, climbing trees, kicking pinecones, and even finding some mushrooms. One of us disturbed a bees' nest and they sent us all slapping and running, our neighbors going as if they would sprint all the way home to Oakland. But they were there waiting when we got back to the car, panting and unstung, and when we got home they accepted our invitation to stay for chanterelle pasta. They surely had never eaten such a thing before, but I think their pride at having been in the field, hunting

and finding wild mushrooms, overcame their reluctance (plus, their dad said they could).

As we all dug in, another boy from the neighborhood stopped in, carrying a fast-food restaurant bag from which he was eating his dinner. My kids looked from burger and bag to me, their faces going from envy to shock to something like fear at what the chef would say. They were expecting maybe a lecture on organic food, multinational corporate greed, and mass-produced "food" and "culture" replacing real food and culture. Maybe it was a teaching moment missed, or maybe it didn't even need the lecture I wasn't up for delivering anyway. Here were children finding delight in eating a meal they had helped to forage and make, that they had seen with their own eyes go from forest to table, meeting and maybe envying a child who was finding delight in a meal he was eating out of an anonymous cartoon-colored bag. I wasn't sure what it all meant, so what I said was, "Want some chanterelle mushrooms to put on that burger?" Yes, he did. Stuffed them in right next to the pickle—forage meets factory. He even shared his fries while the kids bragged about the mushrooms and screamed about the bees. If you can make positive edible mushroom IDs and have a pack of little foragers, use wild mushrooms in this dish. If not, button mushrooms are very good. I like the brown ones called cremini.

Salt

4 tablespoons olive oil or butter, plus more as needed

¾ pound mushrooms, cleaned and sliced

2 garlic cloves, chopped

2 tablespoons chopped parsley

Chopped mint or thyme

2 tablespoons white wine (optional)

2 tablespoons cream (very good)

1 pound spaghetti or fettuccine

Parmesan cheese

Put a big pot of cold water on to boil. Add salt.

Heat a skillet over high heat and add half the oil and then half the mushrooms and ½ teaspoon salt. Toss to coat and cook, stirring occasionally, until the mushrooms are browned and tender when tasted. Set aside and repeat with the other half of the mushrooms. Turn the heat to low, return all the mushrooms to the skillet, and move them to the sides of the pan. To the center of the pan, add a little more oil, if needed, and the garlic, parsley, and mint. Stir the garlic mixture, and when it smells good, stir everything together. Add the wine and then the cream, or a splash of water in place of one of them. Cook the pasta in the salted boiling water, stirring frequently, as you simmer the sauce, adding water if it gets dry. Drain the pasta and stir into the sauce. Taste, correct, and serve with grated Parmesan cheese.

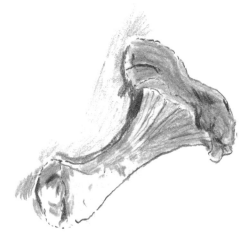

SICILIAN CAULIFLOWER

If you've ever seen it in the field or fresh at the farmers' market, you know that cauliflower grows its own wrapper of dark green leaves that surround the cloudy vegetable as effectively as any cellophane. Why it so rarely shows up in stores in that natural state can probably be answered only by the captains of agribusiness and supermarketry. Rid of its wrap, shiny or leafy, cauliflower dresses up fancy in this pasta with pine nuts, raisins, and, when feeling flush, a gilding of saffron. This Sicilian treatment is sweet, spicy, and satisfyingly complex.

Salt

Olive oil

1 yellow onion, diced

Pinch of saffron threads, crushed to powder with the back of a spoon

Florets from 1 cauliflower head, sliced ¼ inch thick

1 pound bucatini or spaghetti

1 or 2 garlic cloves, chopped

Crushed red pepper flakes

¼ cup dark or golden raisins, soaked in hot water to plump, then drained

¼ cup pine nuts or almonds, toasted tan, not brown (see page 11)

1 teaspoon chopped oregano or marjoram

2 tablespoons chopped parsley

Crumb 2 (page 26)

Parmesan or Pecorino cheese

Put a big pot of cold water on to boil. Add salt.

Heat a skillet over high heat and add 3 tablespoons oil, then the onion, saffron, and a light sprinkle of salt. Stir the onion until it gets going, then lower the heat to medium and cook, stirring occasionally, until soft but not browned, about 15 minutes. Set the onion aside, rinse the skillet to remove any oil or bits of onion that might burn, and put it on high heat. When hot, add 3 tablespoons oil, the cauliflower, and ½ teaspoon salt. Stir to coat the cauliflower but then leave in place to brown. If the skillet seems dry, add a little more oil. When the cauliflower looks and smells good, stir, then leave alone again to get more color. Put the pasta in the pot and stir frequently. When the cauliflower is well browned and tender, turn the heat to low and move it to the perimeter. (Alternatively, you can roast the cauliflower—page 179—and pick up the recipe here.) Add the garlic and red pepper flakes to the center, adding oil if it's dry there. Be careful not to burn it—if the skillet is very hot, wait a minute. When the garlic is just right, bring in the cauliflower and stir around, adding a splash of pasta water if needed for cooling. Add the raisins, pine nuts, oregano, and parsley. Drain the pasta when ready and stir it in. Taste, correct, and serve sprinkled with oily crumbs and grated Parmesan cheese.

If you have half a jar or can of **anchovies** left over from last night's salad dressing, add another savory layer to this pasta and cook them, chopped, in with the garlic and red pepper flakes.

All the colors of cauliflower—white, green, gold—are festive here, or replace half of the cauliflower with **broccoli**.

Many, if not most, people wouldn't even consider eating sardines. If you feel otherwise (I am here to tell you that the little fishes are worth a second look; very fresh ones, for those lucky enough to be near the seas in which they school, are a revelation, but canned can be very deli-cious as well), there's another Sicilian pasta, **pasta con le sarde**,  which basically just replaces the cauliflower with sardines. Wild fennel greens, abundant in Sicily and California, get boiled until tender, chopped, and stirred into the sauce. A teaspoon or so of toasted and ground fennel seeds gives a similar effect.

VEGETABLE CHOW MEIN—ISH

Vegetable chow mein–ish is the dish we cook when we want to eat pasta, but we also want the kids, all of us, to eat lots of vegetables. It's good with the commonest vegetables, such as green beans or broccoli, carrots, and onions, and can adapt to many more. The flavoring can likewise come just from soy sauce, or it can include other bottled Asian ingredients, such as rice vinegar, sesame oil, and hoisin sauce. As the name suggests, I don't claim that this chow mein represents any kind of dish that might be made in China, but for us, it shows up when takeout won't.

3 tablespoons soy sauce

1 tablespoon rice wine vinegar or white wine vinegar

2 teaspoons sesame oil

1 large carrot

4 tablespoons vegetable oil

1 yellow onion, sliced

Scant ½ pound green beans, stemmed and cut into 2-inch

pieces, or florets from 1 broccoli head, sliced ¼ inch thick, or 3 celery stalks, sliced on an angle

½ teaspoon salt

1 pound spaghetti

2 garlic cloves, chopped or thinly sliced

Crushed red pepper flakes (optional)

In a small bowl, mix the soy sauce, vinegar, and sesame oil with ¼ cup of water.

Peel the carrot and cut it into sticks with a chef's knife or by holding it nearly parallel to the side with the biggest holes on a box-type cheese grater. Grate with long strokes and you'll get an easy julienne. Heat a skillet over medium heat and add the vegetable oil, carrot, onion, and green beans. Add the salt and stir. Put the pasta in the pot and stir frequently. When the vegetables are still crisp but trying a little tenderness, turn the heat to low and move them to the sides. Add

a little more oil, if needed, and put the garlic and red pepper flakes (if using) into the middle. Let it sizzle, and when the garlic is cooked, stir everything up and add the sauce mixture. Drain the pasta when ready and stir it in. Taste, correct, and serve.

Keep the onion and carrot, but replace the green beans, broccoli, or celery with **other seasonal vegetables**, such as sliced asparagus, snap or snow peas, bell peppers, spinach, napa or savoy cabbage, button mushrooms, or zucchini.

Add toasted sesame seeds, a spoonful of hoisin or oyster sauce, or a splash of Shaoxing wine to the sauce mixture.

Add **sliced flat omelets** (page 39), **tofu**, or **leftover chopped-up meats** to Vegetable Chow Mein–ish.

Use spaghettini or rice noodles cooked according to package instructions and make this into **curried Singapore shticks**: Add ½ cup roughly chopped cilantro leaves and stems with the garlic. Omit the bottled sauces and replace them with 2½ tablespoons curry powder (or any combination of ground cumin, coriander, clove, fennel, black pepper, paprika, cayenne, and turmeric—the turmeric gives curry its distinctive color, so is best not left out) stirred with 3 or 4 tablespoons water. A little minced ginger is good cooked in with the garlic, and a squeeze of lime to finish brightens it up.

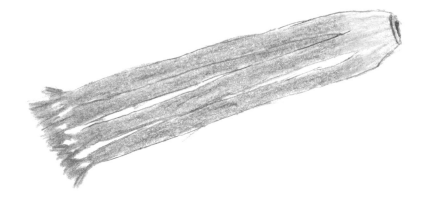

7

RICE, POLENTA, AND MASHED POTATOES

I stand by the rightness of sometimes just having bowls of rice, polenta, or mashed potatoes for dinner. Not often, but they surely feed you better than sugary bowls of venerable, vacuous Cap'n Crunch. In addition to the much-appreciated support that these starches lend to braises and roasts, sticking dinner to plate and rib, they also make champion leftovers, fry-ups, and breakfast boosts.

rice

Rice cooking has always spooked me for some reason. When asked for guidance, cheffy friends with mastery of the skill speak of obsessive washings, electric Japanese rice-cooking machines, and water-to-rice measurements that involved vague finger-knuckle ratios. One friend, traveling in Japan, even shipped home a stout cast-iron wood-fired rice-cooking stove that reportedly made the very best rice. I didn't doubt it, but I was looking for a simpler way that didn't involve splitting firewood or performing underwater massage. What a relief it was, then, when I found out that it's okay to just boil rice in plenty of salted water, like pasta. That's how my

Iranian and Indian friends do it, and that's good enough for me. As with pasta, it's unnecessary to measure anything, and doneness is determined by simply scooping a few grains from the pot and tasting them.

PLAIN RICE

Water	1¼ cups basmati rice
Salt (about 2 tablespoons)	(makes 4 cups cooked rice,
2 tablespoons olive oil or butter	enough for five)

Put a big pot of cold water on to boil over high heat. Add salt. While the water is coming to a boil, rinse the rice. You can soak it, too, but you don't have to. Add the rice to the boiling water and stir once or twice to avoid sticking. Taste, and when tender but still with a little bite, after about 7 minutes, drain. Let sit in the colander for a minute for all the water to drip away, then put the rice back into the pot with the oil, stir once, cover, and let rest in a warm oven or over a very low burner for 10 minutes. Gently fluff with a couple of forks or a wooden spoon before serving.

Any type of rice can be boiled this way. Cooking times will vary. **Brown rice** works especially well but does, of course, take longer to cook. **Farro**, the Italian grain that is somewhere between wheat and barley, can be cooked and eaten just like rice or allowed to cool and dressed as you would for a bean salad (page 52).

To make **crusty saffron rice**, use a heavy-bottomed pot, such as a Dutch oven, to boil the rice. Drain when a little underdone, after about 6 minutes, and let sit in the colander for a minute to steam and drain completely. Return to the pot and sprinkle with a couple tablespoons of olive oil or, if you're really feeling fancy, melted butter into which you've added ground saffron threads. Whole cardamom pods can be added (and discarded after) in place of saffron to perfume the rice. Return the pot to the stove, cover, and cook over very low heat for 40 minutes, turning the pot every 10 so that it eventually makes a full rotation. Do not uncover or stir the rice during this time; if your burner does not sustain a very low setting, you may need to use a flame tamer to avoid scorching. A delicious, crunchy crust will form on the bottom of the pot. My friend Samin cherishes this "tahdig" so much that she safeguards its formation by taking the extra step of lining the lid with a clean kitchen towel and drilling five finger dents deep into the rice. Her mother taught her that the towel absorbs any steam rising from the rice and prevents droplets from falling back into the pot and imperiling the crusty tahdig. The dents, fun to make, are perhaps steam vents, but the point is that this tahdig is worth nurturing. It's that good. No fighting, kids, or I'll eat it all myself!

RISOTTO

My sons, and especially my wife, love risotto. I like risotto fine, but what *I* love is leftover risotto, particularly when it is made into little pan-fried cakes or deep-fried balls. I first had these stuffed and breaded risotto fritters (called arancini, or "little oranges," for their shape and sunny color) when one was handed to me through the window of the Sicily-bound train I was on. It was crisp, golden, and filled with a spoonful of beef stew with little green peas. I learned two important lessons as the train rolled out of the station

that day and I held the now-empty square of grease-spotted paper, savoring the last saffron-scented bite: risotto is well worth making, even if only for the leftovers, and only a fool buys just one arancino.

If there's one rule that should go unbroken in this book and in your kitchen, it is this: never use stock from a can or a carton, for anything, especially for making risotto. If you don't have homemade chicken stock, cook your rice another way. Chicken stock is inexpensive and easy to make (page 206), and though it takes several hours, it's all away-from-the-stove cooking time. If you must have risotto tonight but have no homemade stock, use water, please.

This recipe makes too much risotto, which is ideal for leftover-loving me. It can be halved if for some reason you don't want any leftovers, though I honestly cannot imagine why you wouldn't. Beginning a fast? Final supper? Leaving town first thing? Even if you are, you'll want to take a nice arancino for the ride, no, *caro mio?*

---

1 tablespoon olive oil

4 tablespoons (½ stick) butter

1 yellow onion, diced

Salt

2 cups short-grained Italian rice, such as Arborio or Carnaroli (I have also made good risotto with short-grained Japanese rice)

¾ cup dry white wine

5 cups chicken stock (page 206), hot

¾ cup grated Parmesan cheese

2 tablespoons chopped parsley

Heat a skillet over medium-low heat and add the oil and 2 tablespoons of the butter. When the butter has melted, add the onion and ½ teaspoon of salt and stir. Cook until the onion is soft but not browned, about 15 minutes. Raise the heat to medium-high and add the rice and another ½ teaspoon salt and cook to toast the rice a little, stirring frequently, for 2 minutes. Add the wine, let it bubble for a minute, and then add 1 cup of the hot chicken stock. Keep the skillet at a lively simmer and stir to keep it from sticking. When the liquid is nearly gone, add another cup of stock. Repeat the additions of stock, stirring and tasting for doneness and salt as you go. When the rice is tender but still has a little bite, it's done—about 20 minutes after the wine went in. The risotto should be quite moist, so if it seems dry at all, add a splash more stock or water. Turn off the heat, add the remaining 2 tablespoons butter and the cheese, and stir energetically for 15 seconds. Cover the pan and let it sit off the heat to gather itself for a couple of minutes. Stir in the parsley and serve.

If you are fancy enough to have some saffron and intrepid enough to find beef bone marrow, you can make the classic **risotto alla Milanese**. Let the marrow bones (three 2-inch segments should yield a couple tablespoons of marrow) come to room temperature. Using your finger or the handle of a wooden spoon, pop the marrow from the bones and let it soak in cool water for an hour. Crush the saffron to powder (I use the back of a spoon on a saucer, then rinse the saucer and spoon with the wine to get every speck of precious saffron; too much saffron tastes medicinal, so start with just a few threads) and add with the wine. Push the room-temperature marrow through a sieve and add with the butter at the end. Makes you feel rich in every way, so don't eat too much at a sitting.

Risi e bisi—or risotto with peas—is, like many Italian dishes, as delicious as it is fun to say. Add peas for the last 5 or so minutes of cooking. Depending on the sweetness and tenderness of the peas, you may need to add them sooner. A more generous final addition of stock will make risi e bisi, as it is often served in Italy, *all'onda*, or wavy. **Asparagus**, cut into little segments, can be added the same way as peas. **Cauliflower**, too, chopped small, though it is better if browned first in a skillet or in the oven (page 179). In summer, grate a **zucchini** or two on the large holes of a box grater, sprinkle with salt, and stir into the risotto with the final stock addition.

Peel and dice **butternut squash**, enough to make 1½ cups. (This is a dangerous operation and I have seen even seasoned cooks suffer the consequences, so take care. Peel the squash with a vegetable peeler and carefully cut it in half so it has flat sides and won't roll away from you. Scoop out the seeds and then cut the squash into ½-inch slices. Cut the slices into sticks and then the sticks into dice. The remaining squash will keep for a long time, wrapped, in the refrigerator.) Add to the skillet with the first dose of stock and the squash will be done when the rice is. Sage is particularly good here, cooked for a minute with the onion, right before adding the wine.

One of my favorite risottos is made with **shrimp** and **tomato**, and despite my preference for leftover risotto, this one is best eaten straightaway. Shrimp stock, beautifully colored and irresistibly aromatic, can be easily and quickly made with the shells. Peel ¾ pound shrimp (smaller are better here). Cut them into thumbnail-size chunks, sprinkle with a little salt, and set aside. Chop a little bit of onion, carrot, celery, and fennel if you have some—you don't need much, a total of about 1 cup—and sauté in a little oil for 8 minutes over medium-low heat. Add a small chopped tomato, if you have it, and cook a couple minutes more. Add the shells and raise the heat to medium-high, stirring, and cook until they turn red and smell good. If you have parsley stems and thyme sprigs and a bay leaf, add them in. Fennel and coriander seeds are good, too. Add a splash of white wine (or not) and 6 cups water. Bring just to a boil, turn the heat to low so the stock is simmering softly, and skim off any foam. Cook for 20 minutes, let sit off the heat for 10 more, then strain. Start the risotto as described above, adding a little ground saffron with the onion if you have some. Add a cup of tomato concassé (page 98) or ¾ cup of grated raw or ½ cup roasted tomato puree with the first shrimp stock addition. Add the cut and seasoned shrimp for the last 5 minutes of cooking. Skip the Parmesan and finish with the butter and some chopped parsley.

Sauté **mushrooms**, wild or tame, set them aside, and carry on with the recipe, stirring them into the risotto with the first dose of stock. Thyme is very good here, cooked for a minute with the onion, right before adding the wine. A warm and wintry risotto for two can be made, late on a cold, stormy night, by soaking a little handful of dried porcini mushrooms in hot water for 10 minutes, chopping and adding them to the onion, and adding the juice (watch for grit at the bottom) with the stock.

Arancini, it turns out, are also good when you're not on a train to Sicily. To make them at home, get your hands wet so the cold risotto doesn't stick, and form balls no bigger than a small orange. Make a tunnel to the center of the ball and stuff in a cube of mozzarella or fontina cheese, or a spoonful of chopped-up leftover braised meat (Chapter 10). Collapse the tunnel to seal in the filling, and roll the ball in an egg white or two that you've stirred with a fork in a small bowl. Roll the ball in dry bread crumbs (Crumb 1, page 26), so that it is completely coated. Let the arancini sit for 15 minutes so the breading sets up, or refrigerate up to overnight. Deep- or shallow-fry (page 177) the arancini until nicely browned and heated through, about 4 minutes. When filled with cheese, these are called supplì al telefono, for the way the melty cheese makes strings when the hot risotto ball is pulled apart like telephone lines. Hello, Italy? Just calling to say thanks.

Arancini are good hot, warm, or cool and are good to go.

Yet another of leftover risotto's beloved encores is **riso al salto**, little cakes of risotto that are pan-fried so that the exterior is crispy and the inside is soft like, well, risotto. Simply form cakes of cold risotto with wet hands while a skillet (cast iron really makes things easier) heats to medium on the stove. Add a generous coating of vegetable or light olive oil and place the cakes in the pan, leaving a little room for flipping them over. Let them go for a while—trying to turn the cakes too soon can be disastrous. When you see that they are getting well browned around the edges, slide a spatula under and carefully turn them, one by one. Brown the other side and serve with boiled (page 171) or roasted (page 179) vegetables, Sautéed Greens (page 190), or a leafy salad.

There is a Spanish dish, fideus, which is made by toasting uncooked spaghetti and then simmering it with wine and stock, like risotto. I love eating it with shellfish and aïoli (page 249), and though I'd made it plenty of times, I'd never taken it outside of its traditional undersea world until one night when a total lunar eclipse, a pot lost and mushrooms found, and **campfire-pasta-cooked-like-risotto** changed all that:

"The moon will look like a peach," my son reported as he helped shove camping gear into the trunk of our car. Predictions of rain had prompted me to reconsider the campout, but my sons were undeterred. I don't know what they were expecting, but I wondered if they were confusing lunar with solar, or eclipse with éclair—maybe they thought that a vanilla cream–filled sun would be concealed by a thick coating of chocolate. But they'd never asked to go camping before, so I kept my mouth shut and packed them, a skillet, flashlights, and extra pairs of dry socks into the car and headed for the woods.

That night, glimpses through the mist of the pale and, as promised, peach-colored moon went partway to compensate for damp firewood and a leaky tent. But it was our dinner, foraged in the rain and conjured from our ingenuity, that had us thanking the weather and the boys' persistence: earlier in the day, during our one drizzly forced march of a hike, we'd found chanterelle mushrooms, lots of them, hiding sodden in the oak duff. Back at our campsite, hungry and with paws full of soggy mushrooms, we realized that our hasty scramble out of the house had left us pasta pot–less. With one skillet, a pound of penne, olive oil, salt, and our found treasures, we set about making dinner. The kids picked leaves, mud, and the odd beetle off the mushrooms as my wife and I encouraged their efforts and opened a bottle of wine that had somehow survived our absentmindedness. When they were clean but still quite wet (the chanterelles, not the kids, who were also wet but stayed quite muddy for at least another day), we sliced them up and added them to the hot pan. Their sizzle soon subsided as they released all the rain they'd been soaking up that winter. This sizzle-cessation is usually an unwelcome sound, heralding disappointingly mushy mushrooms, but that night it quietly announced the creation of the pool of amber liquid we'd been counting on to cook the pasta. Into the skillet went our box of raw penne, several additions of water, and a good dose of olive oil, and 30 minutes later, campfire-pasta-cooked-like-risotto was born, gobbled, and gone.

polenta

There are certain foods so dear to one's heart that it is unthinkable that they could be less so to anyone else's, especially my own kids'! Though the evidence is plainly there—dollops and wedges of golden polenta left on plates untouched—I cannot accept that my sons dislike polenta; they just haven't come around quite yet, but with diligence, they will.

More ratio than recipe, this one is pretty simple. Boil 4 cups of water for every one of polenta that you plan to cook. Add 1½ teaspoons salt and then the polenta, sprinkled in slowly, but not ridiculously so, stirring with a whisk all the while. It shouldn't take more than half a minute to get it all in there. Turn it down right away so molten polenta doesn't plop up onto your hand. Switch to a wooden spoon and stir over very low heat until the

polenta is smooth and just bubbling. Cover partially and cook, stirring occasionally (the oft-recommended constant stirring is unnecessary). Polenta usually takes about 30 minutes to cook, though some stone-ground varieties can take a couple of totally worth-it hours. Taste for salt, too, and when it tastes tender, add at least 2 tablespoons butter and more salt, if needed. One cup of dry polenta cooked this way will make plenty for 5 servings. We usually make more so that we have extra to grill or fry the next day.

To prepare hard polenta for frying or grilling, pour the still hot polenta onto a plate or baking sheet so that it makes a layer about ¾ inch thick. Smooth the top with a wet spoon or spatula, let cool, and then refrigerate.

To grill, cut shapes—squares, sticks, triangles—brush with oil, and place on a hot grill. Polenta tends to be a little sticky, so let it sit till you're sure a little crust has formed before trying to turn it. **Pan-frying** is pretty much the same story: get the skillet hot, add oil, and then add the polenta pieces, leaving them in place till crusty, then turning to fry the other side.

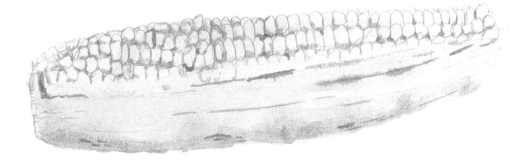

Hard polenta can also be **deep-fried**, and especially luxuriously crisp/soft is polenta that is dusted with all-purpose flour, dipped in egg and then bread crumbs, left to set for a few minutes or hours, and then fried.

Polenta, like its American cousin grits, goes with **cheese**—Parmesan, of course, but also fontina, cheddar, or even a sweet blue. I have enjoyed it for breakfast with a pat of butter or a spoonful of mascarpone on top and sweetened with brown sugar, honey, or maple syrup.

Polenta is a willing sop for **braised meats** (Chapter 10), a comfortable nest for a **poached egg** (page 33), and a soft landing for **vegetables** sautéed or roasted (page 179). **Salsa Verde** (page 244) keeps things interesting.

When **sweet corn** is in full season, shuck 2 ears and cut the kernels from the cobs. I accomplish this by holding the ear upright in a bowl with a kitchen towel folded in the bottom, and cut down with my knife running along the cob. The bowl keeps the kernels from scattering all over, and the towel keeps the knife from striking the bowl, which is harsh treatment for both blade and ear. Simmer the corn kernels in a tablespoon of butter and a couple tablespoons of water with a pinch of salt. Taste, and when tender, stir into the cooked polenta.

In winter, boiled greens or Sautéed Greens (page 190), finely chopped or whizzed in a blender or food processor, can be stirred into the polenta instead of corn. This is called **polenta incatenata**, or "enchained," presumably because it's so beautiful and delicious that you'll be captivated by it.

Polenta can be mixed with good chicken stock (page 206) and sautéed onion to make **polentina**, a simple Italian soup that is especially comforting in gray winter when corn, or anything with a sunny golden warmth, can seem impossibly far away:

Heat a soup pot on high and add 3 tablespoons of olive oil, butter, or rendered duck fat. Add a diced yellow onion and a teaspoon of salt. Stir, lower the heat, and cover the pot with a lid. Check and stir after a few minutes, letting water from the lid drip back into the pot to keep things steamy. If there's any browning going on, turn down the heat and re-cover. Cook like this until the onion is tender, about 15 minutes. Add a couple garlic cloves, chopped or sliced very thin, and stir for a minute. Add 2 quarts of chicken stock, raise the heat to high, and bring to a boil. Lower the heat to a simmer and whisk in ½ cup polenta. Stir until the polenta grains are suspended in the stock and simmer for 30 minutes, or longer depending on the polenta you are using. Taste for salt and for doneness: the grains of polenta should be soft and the liquid thickened. A cup of red wine, reduced in a pan to ¼ cup, is nice spooned over bowls of polentina with some shavings of Parmesan and a crank of black pepper. Salsa Verde (page 244) and a poached egg (page 33) make it a meal, with a salad or Sautéed Greens (page 190) alongside.

The French version, **gaude**, is made the same way, except that the dry polenta is first roasted on a baking sheet in a 350°F oven until aromatic and lightly browned for extra toasty comfort. Sometimes cream or crème fraîche is stirred into gaude just before serving.

mashed potatoes

Mashed potatoes hold a powerful nostalgia for many. My sons feel it not only while the gravy or butter pools golden in the crater but also, and maybe even more strongly, the next morning as they pan-fry patties to eat with eggs. For most of us, the adoration of the mash wanes somewhat in adulthood. For my elderly father-in-law, Bill, on the other hand, it seems to have held, if not grown, and not only for the obvious dental considerations. He is a passionate enthusiast who doesn't eat mashed potatoes every day, but when he does, it is a bad idea to try to stop him. In fact, he claims that his only fistfight was with a mess-hall worker in the army long ago who foolishly refused him a second helping at the steam table. My father-in-law waged a campaign of harassment so sustained that the spud scooper eventually snapped and threw a brick (!) his way—a far greater sin, it seems to me, than stinginess at the potato pot. Bill felt

Boiled potatoes are best left to dry and let off steam for a few minutes before mashing.

so too and gave him a pair of punches, and has peacefully eaten all the mashed potatoes he wants ever since.

I remembered Bill's brief pugilist past when I cautiously agreed to cook a just-the-way-he-likes-it dinner of roasted leg of lamb, mashed potatoes, and gravy for him. I made sure to clear the area of bricks, keep my head down, and allow for plenty of mash. And it must have been okay; I made it through with compliments on the gravy and both eyes unblacked.

For mashed potatoes, you need a floury potato. There are non-waxy yellow varieties to get to know, but the sure-thing spud for mash is the russet. Unless you have an olive oil that you love and are willing to part with a generous amount of, use butter and plenty of it.

Most of the variations on mashed potatoes just complicate things unnecessarily and are best left alone, but in winter, we do like boiling some **celery root**, **parsnips**, **turnips**, or **rutabaga** separately and, after passing them through the food mill, folding them into the mashed potatoes.

---

5 russet potatoes
(about 3 pounds)

1½ tablespoons salt

8 tablespoons (1 stick) butter

½ cup half-and-half or
whole milk

Peel the potatoes and cut in quarters: large chunks absorb less water and yield a richer, more flavorful mash. Rinse them and cover with cold water in a saucepan. Add the salt, bring to a boil over high heat, and then lower the heat to a simmer. Cook until completely tender but not falling apart, about 20 minutes. To be sure they are ready, take a wedge out of the pot and cut it at the thickest part. It should sort of break apart and look dry inside. Tasting a slice will confirm doneness and give you a sense of seasoning. Drain the potatoes and let them sit in the colander to steam and fully drain for a few minutes. Put the pan back on very low heat and add the half-and-half or milk. Set a food mill over the pan and pass a third of the potatoes and a third of the butter through it. Repeat with the rest of the potatoes and butter in batches. Stir the mash just to mix completely; overmixing can result in irrevocable gumminess. Taste and add butter and salt for flavor, half-and-half or milk for texture. Serve straightaway or reheat later, but slowly and carefully—mashed potatoes can stick and scorch.

To make **mashed potato cakes** the next morning to eat with eggs, heat the oven to 400°F and, with slightly wet hands, make patties of mash. Heat the nonstickiest skillet you have to medium-high and add a tablespoon or two of oil. Carefully lay the cakes in the skillet and do not move them. It's pretty difficult to flip mashed potato cakes over in the skillet without their going to pieces, so when they're getting nicely browned around the edges, put the whole skillet (assuming the handle is not meltable) into the oven for 4 or 5 minutes while you cook eggs or make your coffee. Slip a spatula under the cakes and flip them onto plates so that the brown, crispy side is up. Milo really recommends ketchup and hot sauce for mashed potato cakes, though it must be noted that he recommends ketchup and hot sauce, with confidence and no shame, for so many things.

Milo is tickled by fancy-sounding adopted French words—*tête-à-tête, crème de la crème, raconteur, panache* . . . and his personal favorite: *bustier.* They just crack him up for some reason. So when we were in Paris and learned that **shepherd's pie** is called parmentier, well, that was just too *merveilleux*! Which is what our shepherd's pie is, because in addition to the standard meaty stew topped with mashed potatoes, we add a little layer of béchamel sauce. Heat the oven to 425°F and half fill a baking dish, casserole, or cast-iron pan with warm leftover Ragù Finto (page 113) or braised pork (page 222) or chicken (page 212) or duck (page 219), chopped up, with some of the juices. Boiled peas or little cut-up green beans or Sautéed Greens (page 190) are very good stirred in with the meat. Spoon warm Béchamel sauce (page 239), with a little cheese added, over the meat. Spread room-temperature mashed potatoes over, fork them into a whimsical pattern or spoon them into little peaks (or pipe on with a pastry bag or plastic bag with a corner cut off), and bake, uncovered, until browned on top and hot in the middle, about 30 minutes. If the pie doesn't get browned on top, run it under the broiler for a minute, but don't walk away—broilers burn! Safer is to sprinkle the top with oily toasted bread crumbs (Crumb 2, page 26) for color and crunch.

8

VEGETABLES BOILED, ROASTED, SAUTÉED, AND IN SOUPS

As a cook, I am very aware of the seasons as they show themselves through produce. I know when vegetables are in season, but I'm not a farmer, so I don't really know *why* they are in season. It's a mystery, for example, that broccoli and beets seem nearly always to be at the market, looking good. Or that's how they look to me. There are, I'm sure, many who think that they never look good, that eating them is simply out of the question. My happy amazement at beets and broccoli being always in season is, in others, something more like a feeling of betrayal and bitter disappointment, like accepting that freezing sulfurous rain is always in season. The irony barely buried here is an endless three-part cycle of market omnipresence, good-for-you-ness, and popular disgust. I am, I admit, myself haunted by the reek of boiled broccoli that would creep low like mustard gas through the halls of middle school, somewhere between third and fourth period, as netted lunch ladies began their grim work. I am convinced that this, and canned, texture-less pickled beet slices, are the stinky seeds of broccoli and beet discontent, but . . .

Good news! Broccoli and beets, and yes, the entire Family of Earthly Vegetables, are back! And delicious, when cooked right, even by lunch ladies. Cooked right sometimes means simply dropped into a pot of boiling salted water, dipped out when just tender, and dressed with good butter or olive oil and a sprinkle of salt. That's the best way when vegetables are finest and fresh, not coming caged in plastic. Alas, as they are not always so, also offered in this chapter are other ways to cook vegetables right—to do more with lesser stuff.

ONLY-THE-BEST VEGETABLES, BOILED

Though a recipe for boiled vegetables works for nearly any vegetable, when a wise friend advised against it, I chose cauliflower as my subject—not merely to be contrary, but because I suspected that the message motivating that advice was that no one likes boiled cauliflower. This I knew to be untrue in general, but since perhaps accurate when applied to children, I had avoided trying to serve cauliflower to my family. When I would, it was well roasted in a hot oven or sautéed with garlic and Parmesan. I added pine nuts and currants, curry and cilantro, until one day I didn't: a farmer had given me some small perfect heads, no bigger than softballs, pure white and still wrapped in their pale green paisley-shaped leaves. I couldn't bring myself to do anything other than quarter them and boil them, leaves and all, in salted water. Olive oil, a sprinkling more salt, and as we ate them, my son asked, smiling, swallowing, "Have we ever had this before? We should always have it like this."

You may not have farmer friends who are hooking you up with perfect vegetables, but maybe you have a garden yourself or an excellent local market. Either way, at some point, if you are paying attention, there will come along that vegetable that is so clean, so flawless, that you'll know you need only put a pot of water on to boil, adding nothing but a dose of salt. You'll reach for that tiny turnip or cute carrot and it will look up at you and with pale, dewy eyes, ask, "Is my bath ready?"

1 beautifully fresh cauliflower head, preferably organic, probably from a farm near you	Salt
	Butter or olive oil
	Freshly ground black pepper

Cut the cauliflower into florets and taste a little piece raw to make sure that it's all you thought it would be. If not, it's not too late to cook it another way—roasted or in soup? If it's boil-worthy, bring a generous pot of water to a rolling boil and add salt. Taste the water and add more salt until it tastes not like seawater but on its way there—brackish. Drop the cauliflower into the pot. Scoop out a piece after a few minutes and taste for tenderness. When done, after about 4 minutes, scoop out the rest of them, place in a bowl, and dress with the butter or olive oil, salt, and pepper.

Substitute the sweetest, freshest **broccoli, turnips, green beans, snap peas, carrots, celery, fennel, leeks, kale, chard, Brussels sprouts,** or **asparagus** for the cauliflower. **Little potatoes** are good for boiling too, though they take longer. Slip a thin-bladed knife into one to test for tenderness—it should meet little resistance at about 20 minutes for a Ping-Pong-ball-size spud.

Make a Béchamel sauce (page 239) while the boiled vegetables cool, heat the oven to 450°F, and make vegetable gratin (page 240).

Only-the-best vegetables such as cauliflower, green beans, snap peas, carrots, celery, fennel, and asparagus, boiled and then allowed to cool, make great **salads**. See The Undressed (page 78) and Creamy Mustard Dressing (page 89) for how.

Boiled vegetables plus sautéed onion, water, or stock and a blender or whisk equals **vegetable soup**. It's that easy, especially when the produce is good. Heat a soup pot and add 4 tablespoons olive oil, then a sliced

When in top form, vegetables, even humble cauliflower, can move to the head of the table.

yellow onion and a teaspoon of salt. Stir, turn the heat to low, and cover the pot. Check and stir after a few minutes, letting the moisture collected on the lid drip back into the pot to keep things steamy. Lower the heat if there's any browning going on, and re-cover. Cook like this until the onion is very tender, about 15 minutes. Add 2 pounds of roughly chunked vegetables such as cauliflower, carrots, turnips, fennel, or celery to the pot with another teaspoon of salt and water to cover them by a half inch. You can always thin the soup later if it's too thick, so add just enough liquid to cover the vegetables and allow them to bob around a little. Bring to a boil, turn down to a simmer, and cook until the vegetables are very tender. Cooking times vary with vegetables, so taste to determine doneness.

When things are nearly falling apart, eat the soup as it is or crank everything through a food mill or stir meaningfully with a whisk. For a rich, velvety texture that will make even you, the cook who knows better, wonder if there's cream in there, spin it in a blender until completely smooth. Do it in a couple batches, filling the blender less than halfway each time and making sure to hold the lid on while you run the blender so hot soup doesn't spray the walls and you. Add water if it's too thick and won't really get going. You can hear it when it catches and all the soup is being pureed, not just the stuff at the bottom. Let it go for half a minute or so and then pour the soup through a sieve for super-smoothness. Taste and correct for flavor, adding salt or a splash of vinegar or lemon (often welcome) and, for texture, more water or stock if too thick.

If, despite precautions and cautions, your soup is too thin, not to worry, there are fixes. The easiest is with stale bread: Carve off the crust and tear a chunk of bread into little hunks. Put into the blender bowl with some of the soup and let it absorb for a few minutes, until the bread is falling apart. Add a little more soup if needed to get things going and blend until smooth. Stir back into the pot of soup, and repeat if needed. A cup of cooked rice or a cooked potato or two can be used to thicken soup the same way.

When your vegetables are less than perfectly sweet, and you have some chicken stock (page 206), use it in soup. You can also get exotic with these sorts of vegetables and add a few spoonfuls of spices to the cooked onion. Toast a teaspoon each of cumin, coriander, and fennel seeds, grind them, and mix with a teaspoon each of ground turmeric and paprika, and crushed red pepper flakes or cayenne pepper to taste. Stir in with the onions for a minute and add the vegetables. This treatment is especially good with zucchini and corn soup or one made with the roasted tomato purée on page 184 and either roasted chunks of eggplant (page 105) or chunked carrots. Serve with a spoonful of plain yogurt on top.

When you boil vegetables in vinegary brine, you are making **quickles**. Not fermented or processed for keeping, this is a pickle to eat today, tomorrow, or the next day (up to 5 days; keep them refrigerated in the cooled brine they were cooked in). They are only a little harder to make than plain boiled vegetables and, like them, are ready to eat right away once cooled.

½ cup white wine, cider, or red wine vinegar

½ cup white wine

2 teaspoons salt

2 teaspoons sugar

2 bay leaves

1 teaspoon coriander seeds

1 teaspoon fennel seeds

1 teaspoon mustard seeds

½ teaspoon black peppercorns

2 cloves

3 allspice berries

Vegetables (ideas below)

Combine the vinegar, wine, salt, sugar, bay leaves, coriander seeds, fennel seeds, mustard seeds, peppercorns, cloves, and allspice berries in a saucepan with 4 cups water and bring to a boil over high heat. Lower to a simmer and cook for 10 minutes. Taste the brine and see if you want to add more sweetening, salt, or spice. You can leave out the wine if you want and add a little more vinegar. If it tastes too acidic, add water. Cut the vegetables and cook them until tender but still crunchy. Because of the wide variety of possible vegetables, shapes, and sizes, they can take from 5 to 20 minutes, so taste one every few minutes to see. Scoop them out when done and spread on a baking sheet or platter to cool. Cool the brine separately. Reunite brine and pickle if not eating now. The brine can also be used again, diluted as needed with a cup of water.

To pickle: Onions, in rings or wedge-lets . . . carrots many ways, from very thin-cut coins to thick chunks to whole, unpeeled, unwashed babies . . . turnips, sliced or in wedge-lets . . . celery, bias sliced . . . fennel, sliced or in wedge-lets . . . thin coins of zucchini or little florets of cauliflower, with a teaspoon of turmeric brightening the brine . . . red, yellow, and orange pepper rings . . . kernels of corn to mix with chopped pickled peppers and onions for a relish to eat on grilled chicken or fish with tomato salad at a picnic table . . .

To eat: With halved Hard-Boiled Eggs (page 30) . . . on sandwiches . . . over a lettuce salad with avocado dressing (page 91) . . . next to fish smoked, grilled, fried, or baked . . . "I'm with ham" —Pickle . . . chopped into Salsa Verde (page 244) . . . over soft cheese on Thin Crisp Toast (page 20) . . . as part of a salad of cool beans and basil, parsley, or arugula leaves (page 52) . . . "with cold chicken" —Gandalf . . .

I learned this more intuitive way of making **Mexican-style pickles** from the venerable Diana Kennedy. Well, from her cookbooks, anyway. These are the pickled carrots, jalapeños, and onions that I can never get enough of when we're eating tiny tacos from the trucks on International Boulevard in Oakland. I like to rinse the sliced jalapeños under hot tap water for a few minutes to tame their heat and then eat even more of them.

Peel and thickly slice a pound of carrots. Heat a skillet to high and add a couple tablespoons of vegetable or light olive oil and then the carrots, 6 to 8 sliced and rinsed jalapeños, and a yellow, white, or red onion, thickly sliced in rings. Add 2 teaspoons of salt and sauté over high heat for 3 minutes, stirring occasionally. Add ½ cup water, ½ cup cider vinegar, 1½ tablespoons sugar, 1½ teaspoons cumin seeds, and a crumble of dried oregano if you have some. Stir around and simmer for 3 to 5 minutes, depending on how crunchy you like the carrots. Cool and refrigerate in the liquid for up to a week.

Sometimes we decide to boil our vegetables in oil. Also known as fried, vegetables cooked this way have, not surprisingly, considerable appeal. My favorite way to make **fried vegetables** is with my constant companion, yogurt. It's the same idea as frying with buttermilk, and not only is it arguably better tasting, but the leftover yogurt won't languish in the fridge till trash day, the way moldering, half-full cartons of buttermilk tend to. When I'm frying just a little, I use a small cast-iron pan and fill it only halfway with vegetable oil. This method uses less oil, but you have to turn the food to fry the other side: shallow frying. If I'm frying lots and want to go for it, I fill a heavy saucepan, or even a kettle, two-thirds of the way with oil: deep frying.

Either way, while the oil is heating over medium heat (so it doesn't get too hot too fast), put the cut vegetables into a bowl and add enough yogurt to coat the pieces completely. Toss them around with your hands and then roll them in a pan of all-purpose flour. Roll a little ball of what's now coating your fingers and drop it into the oil to test if it's hot enough. Drops to the bottom trailing a thin line of bubbles? Not yet. Foams, spits, and crackles? Too hot; turn it down and wait a few minutes. When it enthusiastically bubbles, the oil is ready. Shake the excess flour off the vegetables and drop them carefully into the oil. Scoop them out when nicely browned, after about 4 minutes, and drain on a rack or on a crumpled newspaper or paper bag. Sprinkle with salt and eat hot.

Cauliflower florets fry up sweet, juicy, and crispy like this. Broccoli, too. Of course slices of onions, separated into rings, are classic fryers, but whole green onions or thin wedges of red onions can be great as well. Rings of sweet peppers, sticks of zucchini, green beans, asparagus, even wedges of Belgian endive heads, cut lengthwise into quarters or sixths, are very good.

Yogurt-frying is also the best and easiest for frying boneless chicken and fillets of fish—same method, just season with salt and pepper before coating.

All fried foods look and smell good with a sprinkle of gremolata (page 246) on them. Not making some sort of mayonnaise—(aïoli, page 249; herby tartar sauce, page 249; even special sauce, page 249) or Salsa Verde (page 244); especially with capers or pickles (page 175) or raita (page 94)—to serve with them would be a foolishly missed opportunity.

JUST PLAIN GOOD VEGETABLES, ROASTED

If what looked like only-the-best cauliflower turns out to be, upon tasting, not so, something can be done: roast it. I am not saying that roasting is just for compromised vegetables: whether with only salt and olive oil, or with complex and assertive spices, roasting can intensify sweetness, caramelize flavors, crisp textures. Roasted vegetables go well with poultry, so we will sometimes decide to roast parsnips and carrots in cold winter, for a comforting Thanksgiving feeling to warm us up. Other times, it's a little burned-around-the-edges texture that we're looking for, so roasting broccoli or Brussels sprouts or even green beans to eat with our bowls of soft polenta or rice is the answer. In summer, zucchini, eggplant, tomatoes, and peppers beg to be roasted into ratatouille the way kids plead for a dip in the lake on a hot afternoon. Most often we'll roast the vegetables for dinner simply because the oven is already lit for another part of the meal and we're feeling frugal, like the family a friend told me about whose oven and water heater were one and the same. He was staying with them in their rustic Scottish country home and one day the family had all gone out. Having the place to himself, he decided to take a hot bath. He was still toweling his wet hair upon their return and was confused by their concern that he'd bathed. "If we'd known you were going to have a bath," they explained, alarmed to have let a hot oven go unoccupied, "we'd have cooked a roast."

1 head cauliflower, florets separated and cut into wedges	2 tablespoons olive oil
	½ teaspoon salt

Heat the oven to 450°F. Dress the cauliflower in a bowl with the oil and salt and toss well to coat. Spread on a baking sheet and when the oven is hot, roast until browned and tender, 15 to 20 minutes.

Broccoli roasts well on its own or in combination with the cauliflower. To roast **winter squash** or pumpkin, carefully cut it in half from top to bottom and scoop out the seeds and stringy stuff. Season the cut sides with salt and rub with oil. Place cut side down on a baking sheet and roast in a 450°F oven until very soft, about 45 minutes. Times will vary with squash size and variety, so test for doneness by inserting a paring knife—it should meet with no resistance. Remove from the oven, and when cool enough to handle, use a large spoon to scoop out the flesh. Stir the roasted squash with salt and plenty of butter, or for a smoother texture, crank through a food mill or whiz in a food processor. Serve with roasted or grilled meats (Chapter 11), braised meats (Chapter 10), or Poached Eggs (page 33) and a sprinkle of cayenne, hot sauce, or harissa (page 63). Make a roasted squash soup as in the recipe for boiled vegetables (page 171), adding cumin and coriander seeds or curry powder to the onion and serving with a dollop of plain yogurt. Mix in equal parts with chickpeas for a colorful and slightly sweeter hummus (page 57). The smaller types of winter squash—Delicata, Acorn—can be cut into slices or wedges, coated with oil, and sprinkled with salt before spreading on a baking sheet and roasting in a 450°F oven until browned and soft, about 15 to 30 minutes. If the skin is tender enough, eat it. If not, eat around it.

Roast squash for puree or soup, or to eat as is in slices or chunks.

Root vegetables are especially good roasters. Carrots, turnips, parsnips, celery root, rutabaga, and Jerusalem artichokes can all be peeled, cut into chunks, tossed with oil and salt, and roasted just like cauliflower. Cook them singly, or if you want to combine several types, pay attention to their density as you cut them: the harder vegetables will take longer to cook through, so you'll want to cut them smaller. Serve roasted roots with roasted or grilled meats or let them cool a bit and toss with escarole, radicchio, or other hearty greens and Shallot and Sherry Vinaigrette (page 88).

Beets are best when roasted, whole and unpeeled. First, cut the greens off the roots and save them, if they're in good shape, for another use (page 190). Rinse the beets and put them in a small baking pan with ¼ inch of water and a sprinkling of salt. Cover the pan with foil and roast in a 450°F oven until a knife meets very little resistance when slipped into the center of a beet, about 1 hour. Remove from the oven, uncover, and set aside to cool. Slip the skins off the beets with your hands, cut them into slices or wedges, and dress with red wine vinegar, olive oil, and salt. (Some people like to wear rubber gloves when peeling red beets, though to me pink fingers are a small price to pay for being able to feel the food I'm cooking.) Eat them warm or refrigerate for up to 3 days. Roasted beets are great surrounding green salads (don't toss them in or they'll turn everything that disturbing blood-red), with sliced avocado and Citrus Zest Vinaigrette (page 93), or with boiled green beans and a dollop of aïoli (page 249). Beets and other roasted vegetables make richly flavored soups   follow the method recommended for making soup with boiled vegetables (page 172).

Like beets, **sweet red or yellow peppers** can also be roasted whole, then peeled and dressed. Rub them with oil and roast in a 450°F oven on an uncovered pan until the skin blisters, about 20 minutes. Leave to cool and steam in a paper bag or covered bowl. They can then be peeled, seeded, and, if need be, rinsed to get rid of charred bits before cutting and dressing with splashes of olive oil and red wine vinegar and a sprinkle

of salt. Chop and mix into Salsa Verde (page 244), slice into strips for bean salads (page 52), or leave in big slabs and eat with goat cheese or ricotta or scattered with olives, capers, and anchovy fillets.

When zucchini and our favorite nightshades—tomatoes, eggplants, and peppers—are ripe, we make **ratatouille**. We start by cooking Summer Marinara (page 103) with roasted eggplant, as for pasta alla Norma (page 105). We stir in peperonata (page 193) and zucchini, either sautéed as for Bibo's Zucchini Pasta (page 131) or roasted in the oven like the eggplant. In a large skillet or wide soup kettle, everything gets combined and simmered until very tender and almost melting together, 30 minutes or longer. After tasting, we might add a splash of red wine vinegar, chopped parsley, maybe even capers or a few chopped anchovy fillets. Great at any temperature, ratatouille is perhaps best served just cool, with a slice of mozzarella or ricotta and a brush of nostalgia.

Depending on how you plan to eat them, there are a couple of ways to roast tomatoes. If you have an abundance of ripe tomatoes and want to make **roasted tomato puree**, heat the oven to 400°F, cut the tomatoes in half or into big chunks, toss with oil and salt in a baking dish or cast-iron pan, and roast them until starting to fall apart, 20 minutes to 1 hour, depending on volume. Crank the roasted tomatoes through a food mill to remove the skins and seeds and you have a basic tomato sauce to use in pasta recipes (Chapter 5), to freeze for later, or to make the following soups.

PAPPA AL POMODORO

½ loaf stale bread, torn or chopped into chunks (Italian rustic white is traditional, but use what you like)

3 tablespoons olive oil, plus more for serving

1 yellow onion, diced

Salt

3 garlic cloves, thinly sliced

Big handful of basil, leaves only, washed, dried, and very roughly chopped

2 cups roasted tomato puree (opposite)

3 cups chicken stock (page 206) or water

Toss the bread with a light coating of olive oil and a bit of salt and crisp in a 400°F oven for 8 to 10 minutes. Meanwhile, heat a soup pot over high heat and add the olive oil and then the onion and a teaspoon of salt. Stir, turn the heat to low, and cover the pot. Check and stir after a few minutes, letting water from the lid drip back into the pot to keep things steamy. Lower the heat if there is any browning going on, and re-cover. Cook like this until the onion is very tender, 15 to 20 minutes. Uncover, raise the heat, and add the garlic and basil. Stir for a couple of minutes and then add the roasted tomato puree and the stock or water. Bring to a low boil and then adjust the heat to low to keep the soup at a simmer and cook for another 20 minutes. Turn off the heat, add the bread, and stir well. Let the pappa al pomodoro sit for at least 15 minutes and then eat with lots of good olive oil poured over. Pappa al pomodoro gets better with age (up to 3 or 4 days, refrigerated; because it's so thick, it should be stirred in the fridge occasionally to speed the cooldown). Thin with water, if necessary, and reheat over medium heat, stirring often, before serving.

ROASTED TOMATO BISQUE WITH FENNEL SEEDS

3 tablespoons olive oil

1 yellow onion, sliced

Salt

3 garlic cloves, chopped

1 teaspoon fennel seeds

Crushed red pepper flakes

½ cup white rice (brown rice can be used but will require longer cooking)

3 cups roasted tomato puree (page 184)

4 cups chicken stock (page 206) or water

Drizzle of extra-virgin olive oil (optional)

Chopped basil or mint (optional)

Crème fraîche, sour cream, or plain yogurt (optional)

Crushed toasted fennel seeds (optional)

Heat a soup pot over high heat and add the olive oil, then the onion and a teaspoon of salt. Stir, turn the heat to low, and cover the pot. Check and stir after a few minutes, letting the moisture collected on the lid drip back into the pot to keep things steamy. Lower the heat if there's any browning going on, and re-cover. Cook like this until the onion is very tender, 15 to 20 minutes. Uncover and add the garlic, fennel seeds, and red pepper flakes. Stir for a minute and then add the rice, roasted tomato puree, and stock. Bring to a low boil and then adjust the heat to keep the soup at a simmer and cook for another 20 minutes. The rice tends to settle and stick to the bottom, where it can scorch, so stir occasionally. Taste a few grains of rice to be sure they are cooked—simmer a bit longer if necessary, until all graininess is gone. Let the bisque cool for 5 minutes, then stir vigorously with a whisk, crank through a food mill, or, for the creamiest result, carefully spin in the blender, filling the container only halfway each time to prevent a hot red tomato shower. Taste for salt, correct, and serve hot, warm, or chilled. If desired, a swirl of extra-virgin olive oil and a sprinkle of chopped basil or mint makes a nice topping, as does a spoonful of crème fraîche, sour cream, or plain yogurt with a few extra crushed fennel seeds.

To make this into **roasted tomato and carrot soup with spices**, add a teaspoon each of cumin and coriander seeds, ground turmeric, and paprika, and crushed red pepper flakes to taste. Use only 2 cups of roasted tomato puree (page 184) and add 3 large carrots, chunkily sliced, in with it. Simmer until the carrots and rice are very soft, about 30 minutes, but taste to be sure. Whisk, crank, or spin as opposite. Taste, and thin as needed.

The best variety for **stuffed and roasted tomatoes** (see pages 188–89) is Early Girls, little single-serving tomatoes that are the size of lemons, but any type can be stuffed like this. Cut the tops off, going in shallow and wide with your knife, removing the caps so that the tomatoes look like mini red pumpkins ready for carving. Squeeze the tomatoes, holding them upside down over a dish, just hard enough to get some of the seeds and juice out and to make room for the herb stuffing. Sprinkle a little salt into them and then top with a spoonful of Salsa Verde (page 244). Simple parsley-garlic salsa is pretty perfect, but other fresh herbs, like marjoram, oregano, or basil, fit well. Capers and olives dive right in, too. Sometimes I add a little bit of bread crumbs (Crumb 2, page 26) to the stuffing to make it more substantial. Push the stuffing down into the cavity a little, set the stuffed tomatoes in a baking dish or small skillet that fits snugly enough to hold them upright, and bake at 375°F until very soft but still holding their shape, about 45 minutes. They look impressive and beautiful on the plate, and then turn into herby tomato sauce as you cut into them and start eating. Serve alongside any meats (Chapters 9 and 10), a spoonful of Polenta (page 158), or with Poached Eggs (page 33) and a salad (Chapter 4).

SAUTÉED GREENS

There's a good reason that the sauté position is the top spot at Chez Panisse and in most restaurant kitchens: in addition to fielding orders and corralling the cooks so that the food all comes up together, the sauté cook also has to actually sauté, and sautéing can be tricky. It's the open-pan, real-time, not-burning, sauce-making intensity of aggressively browning, say, squid tentacles while gently browning fragile fish fillets, and blooming the garlic before tossing in green beans while cooking the onions, mushrooms, and fresh herbs, in the right order, with the right consistency to coat but not drown the pasta. It's happening all at the same time: intense, and not for everyone. But at home it's a very different story. The open-pan, real-time aspects still excite, but now also offer clarity—it's all right there, no vegetables hiding beneath boiling waters or closed in hot ovens—and you are able to immediately see, hear, smell, touch, and, of course, taste the food as it cooks.

All but the hardest of vegetables can be sautéed, and it's the preferred method with many green vegetables, especially leafy greens.

---

1 bunch rapini, aka broccoli rabe, or other leafy greens (see page 192)	2 garlic cloves, finely chopped (optional)
Olive oil	Crushed red pepper flakes (optional)
Salt	

Start chopping the stem ends of the rapini bunch, cutting them small and getting larger as you move toward the flower end. Throw it all into a big bowl of water and swish it around to get rid of any dirt. Dip out the greens into a colander (don't pour them out or the dirt will just go right back on), but do not spin them dry—it's good to have some water clinging to the leaves to help them steamily cook. Heat a skillet to medium-high; add the oil and then the rapini and salt. Let it begin to wilt and then turn things around with tongs,

getting the top leaves to the bottom. Cook for 10 minutes, adding a splash of water if things sound sizzly, and then taste a leaf and a stem for both tenderness and seasoning. Cook more if needed, adding salt, oil, or water as needed. When the greens are tender, move them to the perimeter and, if you're adding garlic and red pepper flakes, and I think you should, put them center-skillet, adding oil if it's dry there. When the garlic smells just right, bring in the rapini and stir around, adding a splash of water if needed to prevent burning.

Substitute **spinach**, **chard**, **beet greens**, or **kale** leaves stripped off their stems or any other leafy green. If the skillet starts to get sizzly before the greens are cooked (kale especially can take a while), add splashes of water until they are tender.

Sautéed greens make my favorite kind of **Frittata** (page 40).

The first time I had **peperonata** was at a county fair, spooned over a griddled sausage sandwich I was eating between 4-H events on a summer afternoon. It wasn't called peperonata, of course; it was just peppers and onions that had been sizzling away—sautéing—in the fat from the coils of sausage with which they were sharing space on a midway flat-top. I was hooked right away, and pleased when I discovered, years later, that there was such a nice Italian name for it. When I make it now, I slice up a colorful mix of bell peppers, tasting them raw to gauge the sweetness and the proportion of onions needed. Usually I use 2 parts peppers to 1 part onions, but if the peppers need a little help, I slice them in equal amounts. Either red or yellow onions will work fine, yellow ones cooking up sweeter. Heat a skillet to medium and add olive oil, the onions and peppers, and a sprinkle of salt. Stir well to coat and cook, stirring occasionally, until both peppers and onions are very tender and sweet, about 20 minutes. Use the same technique as for Sautéed Greens (page 190) to add in garlic and hot red pepper, if you like. A splash of red wine vinegar is often in order, and capers are good as well. County fair or no county fair, peperonata is a natural with sausages and, for that matter, any grilled meat, fish, or Polenta (page 158). A valuable leftover, peperonata is very good with a fried egg (page 37) or in piperade (page 37) for breakfast, and it makes a great, if messy, sandwich with cheese or cold sliced meats.

Peperonata can be turned easily into **sweet pepper bisque** (a bisque is a soup that is thickened with rice) simply by adding a small handful of rice once the onions and peppers are cooked, plus either water or stock to cover by half an inch. Bring to a boil, lower the heat to a simmer, and cook until the rice is very tender. Spin in a blender (carefully, especially if it's still hot), in batches, adding more water or stock to thin as needed, and pass through a sieve for extra smoothness.

Once, back on the farm, my mother surreptitiously roasted a beef heart for family dinner, the defrosted dregs of a half side of beef my parents had signed up for: frozen cuts wrapped in white paper, labeled with Magic Marker and stored in a coffin-shaped freezer in our dark, wet basement. She felt clever and frugal with her mystery roast and, I imagine, at least a little deceitful as my father, brother, sister, and I tucked in, praising the dense but tender meat and the rich, dark gravy. When our plates were licked clean and her—forgive me—offal secret was revealed, it was a bit of an anticlimax: still reveling in how delicious it was, we weren't nearly as appalled as she thought we'd be. Heart roast didn't exactly become a family tradition, but oh, that bloody good gravy.

I, on the other hand, set out to deceive no one when I fried little balls of Sautéed Greens (page 190) mixed with stale bread and onions for a family snack one evening. Later, receiving compliments on how tender and delicious the *meat*balls were, I realized the deception had taken place. These were vegetarian meatballs—not because anyone needed them to be, but because they tasted so good just like that. Mine was a victimless crime, as my mother's had been (discounting, of course, the original owner of that football-size heart), and like hers, the evidence was destroyed quickly and with pleasure.

FRIED GREENS MEAT*LESS*BALLS

3 tablespoons olive oil

1 small yellow onion, diced

Salt

2 garlic cloves, chopped

½ cup roughly chopped cilantro

1 tablespoon cumin seeds

1 bunch chard or kale, washed and sautéed until tender and then chopped fine

1 cup stale bread crumbs (Crumb 1, page 26), fine or a little chunky

2 eggs

¼ cup crumbled feta

All-purpose flour, for dredging

Oil, for frying

Heat a skillet over medium-low heat and add the oil, onion, and salt. Cook, stirring occasionally, until soft and lightly browned, about 10 minutes. Add the garlic, cilantro, and cumin seeds, stir for 30 seconds, and then turn the mixture out into a large bowl. Let cool for 5 minutes and then add the chard, bread crumbs, eggs, and feta. Mix with your hands until completely combined. Make a little ball or patty, dip it into the flour, pat off the excess, and either deep- or shallow-fry it (see page 177 for more on frying). Cool for a minute and taste. Make any corrections needed for flavor or texture (more egg or a splash of water if too dry; more bread crumbs if too wet), and then form, flour, and fry the rest.

Hot fried little meatlessballs, the size of a cherry, make a nice snack or appetizer to pass around. You can also make them bigger, replace the cumin with **fennel seeds** and the cilantro with **basil or oregano**, and eat them simmered in marinara sauce (Summer, page 103, or Not-Summer, page 106) and tossed with pasta. They make a good lunch or dinner served with some **boiled** (page 171) **or roasted** (page 179) **vegetables** or a salad (Chapter 4), with a spoonful or two of yogurt as a sauce. These fritters are also good later, to eat at room temperature out of hand and on the go.

9

ROASTED CHICKEN

"Because it was being roasted in the back of a truck" is the tastiest answer I've heard yet to that puzzling, oft-asked question. And it may be that to get across the road is in fact why the chicken was being roasted in the back of a truck. More likely it's because of the crisp skin and tender meat created by those stacked series of spits that encourage the fat from the chicken above to drip onto his downstairs neighbors—gravity basting. Perhaps the messiness of the hot-oven technique I settled on while trying to re-create that superior quality in my stationary, rotisserie-free kitchen is also the key to its success: the skin crisps while the fat renders and spatters, little droplets flying up and landing back on the bird—shower basting. Greasy oven, sure, and a little smoke, but a delicious result. I'm now experimenting further with positioning my smoke detector at just the right distance from the oven so that when it blares, dinner is served.

SMOKE ALARM/DINNER BELL CHICKEN

Take the chicken out of the refrigerator at least 1 hour and up to 3 hours before roasting. If there are giblets in there, take them out—the neck is good for stock making, and I like the other bits for other purposes—the liver to sauté for a snack, the heart and gizzard to braise and chop into gravy (page 205)—but you don't have to. If the chicken seems wet, blot it dry with a paper towel. Place it breast up in a shallow-sided baking dish, like a casserole, and season it with lots of salt and black pepper, inside and out and all around. Your hands are now all chickeny, so either wash them or ask a friend to pour a couple tablespoons of oil on, then rub it all over the chicken skin. For a neat look, tuck the wings up behind the neck so that it looks like it's kicking back. If you have some string that won't melt in the oven (kite string, gardening twine, anything that's clean and not plastic), tie the ends of the legs together. Wash your hands and do something else while the chicken comes to room temperature.

Preheat the oven to 450°F 15 minutes before you're going to roast so it gets good and hot. Put the chicken in the oven. (At this point, I unplug the battery in my smoke alarm, and maybe you should, too, but remember to plug it back in, please. Maybe set a timer, not for the chicken, but so that you won't forget to turn the smoke alarm back on and I won't have to worry.) Roasting hot like this, the fat tends to spatter and make a smoky situation that is totally worth it. Check it in 45 minutes: take it out of the oven and grab the end of one of the drumsticks with your hand in a kitchen towel. Twist the leg. It's done if the bone turns easily, independent of the meat. If it still feels tight, roast it some more. Another way to check is to cut the skin between the thigh and the body, bend the leg/thigh away from the body, and peek to see how it looks at the joint. If it's reddish, and when poked with a knife tip, the juice runs pink, it's not done. When it looks light pink or white and the juice is running clear, done.

To cut up a roasted chicken, start by taking off the leg/thighs. Disassembling the roasted bird in the pan makes for a much less messy operation, but have a cutting board at hand for slicing the parts as you take them off the carcass. With the chicken's tail toward you, cut through the skin between the thigh and the body and bend the legs away from the body of the bird. The thigh is attached to the body just at the hip joint, so you should be cutting only through skin. Down at the bird's backbone is where the ball of the thighbone fits into the hip socket. It can be hard to find, but poke around with your knife tip, tilting the thigh away from

the body, and you'll get it. Cut the cartilage around the joint, pull the leg down and away, and then cut through the skin along the back and the leg/thigh should come away. Place it on a cutting board and separate the drumstick from the thigh by cutting where they meet. You're not cutting through bone, just the cartilage around the joint. Sometimes I will cut the thigh part in half—lengthwise, right along the bone—if it's an especially large chicken or I just want more pieces to serve. Do the other leg and then the breasts: Right down the middle there is a bony ridge called the keel bone, like the keel of a boat. Make 2 cuts close in on either side of this bone, from the neck toward the tail. Using your fingers, or a fork if it's too hot, pull the breast meat away from the body and follow down the curve of the bones with your knife. Near the neck you're following the wishbone and, farther down, the rib cage. Pull back the meat as you go and when it's all away, cut through any skin still holding it and place the breast on the cutting board. Slice it across into 3 or 4 pieces,

trying to keep some of the skin with each slice. Do the other side and keep warm until you're ready to serve. Don't forget the wings and the succulent oysters that nestle in along either side of the backbone.

Eating pieces of chicken while carving is an honored tradition that, if not required, is certainly recommended. My dad used to set aside prized nuggets, asking us to keep watch on them while they cooled so that he could taste and make sure it was good enough. When he looked away, we'd pop them into our mouths and run, chewing and giggling, as he pretended to be shocked that they'd gone missing.

"Did you see anyone take that?" he'd ask.

"Nope," we'd squeak through a mouthful, delighted. Still works.

I'm not much of a cardplayer, so I haven't been able to use poker as a parenting matrix through which to teach my kids about life's behavioral bluffs and personal politics—hold 'em and fold 'em, and all that wisdom Kenny deals. But on the kitchen table, as on the gaming table and in life, there *are* decisions to make, choices that weren't there when you started. Better to cook the thing gloriously whole or in little manageable pieces? Carefully or with arms thrown wide? With pride? With hunger? In love? Sometimes you don't need to set it on fire to get it right. Sometimes you want to be more discreet, to maybe not send up the big smoke signal. That's when to make **cast-iron-pan-roasted chicken**. What is perhaps lost in crispiness and color is, arguably, offset by gains in juiciness and texture. Heat the oven to 475°F and put a cast-iron pan in there. Prepare the chicken as described above, and when the oven and pan are hot and the bird seasoned and oiled, carefully slip it in. Turn off the oven after 20 minutes. Don't open the door and peek, have faith, and the chicken will be done 30 minutes later. This is for a 3½- to 4-pound chicken—bigger or smaller, adjust the oven-off time by 5 minutes.

Hearts and gizzards can be seasoned and simmered in a little stock and wine to be chopped up and mixed into Bolognese sauce (page 115) or into gravy.

A simple **gravy** can be made from the fat, juices, and browned bits left in the roasting pan. Scrape it all together and pour off into a small, deep bowl or a cup. Add a little water or stock to the pan to rinse out anything left behind and add it to the bowl. Discard any large pieces of skin or bone. Let the fat rise to the top for 5 minutes and skim off as much as you can with a small ladle or a large soupspoon. Put a big tablespoon of the fat into a small saucepan to make the roux; the rest of the fat you can get rid of. Add a tablespoon of all-purpose flour to the fat and cook, whisking, over low heat for 3 minutes. Start whisking in the remaining roasting juices, as for Béchamel sauce (page 239), and when it's all in, raise the heat to bring to a simmer, whisking all the while. If you want more gravy, start with a bit more fat and flour and add extra stock or milk with the pan juices. A little white wine or sherry, or even a drop or two of sherry vinegar, make nice additions. A spicy dose of ground black pepper is often a good idea. Bring to a boil, turn the heat to a low simmer, and let the gravy cook for 5 minutes. Taste and adjust for flavor as well as thickness.

No one needs to be told that mashed potatoes are good with roasted chicken, especially if you've made gravy, but you may not have thought to **roast little potatoes** right in the same pan with the bird. Use small yellow-fleshed potatoes or cut bigger ones into chunks, toss them with some salt, and add them to the roasting pan 15 minutes after placing it in the oven. Stir them around occasionally to coat with the chicken fat. They should be done right when the chicken is. If you love garlic, break some whole cloves off a head and toss them, unpeeled, with the potatoes.

The soft roasted garlic slips easily from the skins when cooked and tastes great smeared on everything.

Stuff the chicken with a mixture of Rustic Oily Croutons (page 25), sautéed onions and celery, parsley, sage, and Sautéed Greens (page 190) or mushrooms. Moisten the **stuffing** with a little stock if you have it, or water if you don't. A little cooked bacon or sausage is heartily good mixed in. A chicken so stuffed will take a little longer to cook.

Once you've eaten all the meat from the carcass, make stock with it. The bones of a roasted chicken make a fine stock, especially for soup, since it is already seasoned, but I also like to make **chicken stock** from raw, unseasoned bones—it has a cleaner and fuller flavor, and is better for making risotto. The method is the same either way: The bones go into a pot with a halved onion, a big carrot, and a stalk or two of celery. If you don't have carrot or celery, that's fine, but the onion is pretty essential. Add also a couple sprigs or stems of parsley and thyme and a bay leaf. Cover with cold water by 4 or 5 inches and bring to a boil over high heat. Immediately turn down to a simmer and skim off the foam that rises to the surface. Keep at a low simmer for 3 hours, then strain. Allow the stock to sit for 5 minutes, and then skim off the fat with a ladle. If you aren't cooking with the stock right away, refrigerate, uncovered, until cold. Freeze chicken stock in quart or pint containers and it will come in so handy later.

10

In our family, we abide by the common household rule that the one doing the cooking need not do the cleaning up. In an effort to leave a less than FEMA grade disaster for someone to deal with, I look for one-pan dishes to cook. So it was a real breakthrough moment for me when I learned that I could do a braise entirely in the oven, skipping the messy, perilous pan-browning start that I'd always thought was so crucial. With simple heat regulation and short intervals of careful turning and tending, long and slow braising in the oven yields meat as tender, juicy, and caramel-colored as the venerable flour-and-brown topside technique.

Now I use both methods and have picked up a third: boil and grill. I'm assigning a meat to each method in the recipes that follow, but they are interchangeable: all methods work with all meats. Deciding when to cook what and how depends on factors that include your desire for a certain effect (light and saucy, rich and stewy, smoky grilled or oven crisped), ingredients available (duck, chicken, pork), equipment available (stove-

top, oven, grill, cleanup buddy, funds), how much time you have, and how much of it you're eager to spend in the kitchen. You are encouraged to switch up the recipes and the suggested accompaniments and to simmer up your own.

The best parts to braise are the tougher ones, the ones that won't roast, grill, or pan-fry to tenderness. From the four-legged herd, this means shoulder and belly cuts. From the feathered flock, the legs and wings (and neck: my nana used to wallow in Thanksgiving martyrdom, standing by the hot stove, complaining happily through mouthfuls, "Oh, I'll just have the neck of the turkey; that's good enough for old Nana. You all go ahead and sit without me." It wasn't just the pity that she relished: that neck was *tasty* after a long, slow simmer in the fat and juices of our holiday bird. She did sit down to dinner with the family, of course, and after pie she'd continue, "I'll just do all the cleaning up before another sleepless night on my bed of nails." It was all show—she ate and slept and was up in the morning with a fragrant pan of cinnamon rolls waiting for us hot from the oven. I credit that lovely woman with planting the seeds that grew into my career as a chef.)

Braised meats are the favorite of many a smart cook, and not only because they bubble up tender and moist and make their own flavorful sauce in the process, but because they are less expensive to boot.

Pork shoulder, duck legs, and chicken thighs are my favorites for braising at home. Lamb shoulders and shanks, beef short ribs, oxtails, and chuck-eye make fine braises, too, and all braised meats make versatile leftovers, often getting even better when refrigerated for a day or two. I like braises also for their make-ahead-ability and long, mostly unattended cooking time: you can do something else as they simmer—go for a walk, read a book, write a letter—and know that all the while, you're making dinner. So virtuous!

Serve braised meats with a ladleful of the liquid they were cooked in. If there's any liquid left, save it for soup making.

BRAISED CHICKEN LEGS

There are two steps in the braising process: the tasty browning and the tender cooking. Here the chicken is browned in a skillet first, then cooked to tenderness either in the oven or on the stovetop. Dusting the seasoned meat with all-purpose flour thickens the braising liquid and results in a rich, gravy-like sauce. Using stock will give you the most flavorful dish, but water really does work well, especially if you help it out with plenty of flavor from spices and fresh herbs. Wine gives the stew roundness, complexity, and welcome acidity. Beer-cooked chicken has roots in Europe as well as in China and the Americas and renders an earthy, grainy, bitter/fruity flavor, depending on the type of beer used.

The onion can stand alone if you don't have the carrots and celery, but get some for next time—they are so good in so many things and when in the sweet midst of their individual seasons, each can step forward from the trio and take their solo.

5 chicken legs (drumstick and thigh together)

1½ teaspoons salt

Freshly ground black pepper

All-purpose flour, for dredging

4 tablespoons vegetable oil or butter

¾ cup white or red wine, beer, chicken stock (page 206), or water

1 yellow onion, diced

1 large carrot, diced

2 celery stalks, diced

2 garlic cloves, chunked, chopped, or sliced

Roughly chopped leaves from 3 thyme, rosemary, or sage sprigs

1 bay leaf

3 cups chicken stock (page 206) or water

Finely chopped leaves from 6 parsley sprigs

Season the chicken legs well with 1 teaspoon each of the salt and pepper and let them sit for a while, 15 minutes to an hour (or, best, over-night in the refrigerator to absorb the seasoning). Unless you're cooking in the tropics or there's a hungry, ill-trained dog capable of counter jump-ing, they need not be refrigerated. Leash that dog and dredge the chicken legs: Put the flour into a bowl or, better, a deep cake pan (the high sides make for less flour-dusting of the kitchen floor), add the chicken legs, and tumble them around so they get completely coated. Shake off all excess flour or it will burn in the skillet and that greasy burned-toast smell will stick. Don't flour more than you can fry at a go, so depending on the size of your skillet, you may have to work in batches. Heat a skillet over high and when it's nice and hot but not smoking, add 2 tablespoons of the oil and then, pretty quickly, the legs. This is an important part: if you leave the oil alone in the hot skillet for long, it will burn and give the braise an off taste. So carefully but swiftly place the floured legs in the hot oil and adjust the heat so that they're sizzling nicely, not ferociously. Leave them in place; don't move them any more than needed to make them fit snugly in the skillet. Add more oil if it looks dry. When you can see them getting brown around the edges, after about 5 minutes, turn them over. You're not trying to cook them through at this stage, so when they are browned all over, about 3 minutes more, set the legs aside. Turn off the heat under the skillet and turn the oven on to 450°F.

Unless it looks too dark and burned, it's time to add some liquid to simmer up all the sweet and flavorful bits that are sticking to the skillet. First pour off all the grease and then return the skillet to medium heat and deglaze by adding the wine and scraping with a wooden spoon as it bub-bles. When it's all dissolved and dislodged, pour the deglazing liquid into a bowl and set aside. (If the skillet is in fact too burned, just wash it out and skip the deglazing step, adding the wine later when the legs go back in.) Add the remaining 2 tablespoons oil, the onion, carrot, and celery, and the remaining ½ teaspoon salt. Cook for 10 minutes, stirring occasionally. Add the garlic, thyme, and bay leaf and cook for a minute, and then return the chicken to the pan, skin side up, along with the reserved deglazing liquid and stock or water. Bring to a simmer and put the skillet in the oven. After 5 minutes, lower the heat to 325°F. (Or you can skip the oven and simmer, covered loosely, on a low burner.) Cook until very tender, 30 to 40 minutes. Test for doneness by inserting a slender-bladed knife into the meat. It should pull out easily with very little grab. If the knife sticks, cook for 10 minutes more. Check again, and when done, remove from the oven, lift the legs from the skillet, and set them aside. Pour the contents of the skillet into a small, deep-sided bowl to allow the fat to rise for 5 minutes. With a small ladle, skim off the floating grease layer. Recombine the braising liquid and vegetables with the chicken skin side up, bring back to a simmer, and pop back into the oven for 5 minutes. Sprinkle with the chopped parsley, and eat right away, or save to reheat later.

Chicken cooked in red wine—**coq au vin**—I think of as the classic of classics. To make it, add some sliced-up bacon when the legs first go back in the skillet and braise with red wine replacing all the liquid or with a combination of plenty of red wine and stock or water. Coq au vin is comforting in the winter with the carrots cut chunky and served with mashed potatoes (page 162) or other mashed roots and scattered with parsley and Rustic Oily Croutons (page 25).

In summer, **chicken legs braised with paprika** is seasonally colorful and delicious. Uncover the skillet for the last 10 minutes of cooking and make a paste with 1 teaspoon sweet paprika and a couple spoonfuls of the braising liquid. Brush up the legs so that they're all red and fragrant and continue cooking. Serve with chickpeas and peperonata (page 193), and pass simple parsley and garlic Salsa Verde (page 244) at the table.

In addition to salt and pepper, season the legs with cumin, corian-der, paprika, and a little cinnamon and caraway for a **Moroccan-scented braise**. Substitute ¼ cup roughly chopped cilantro stems and leaves for the other herbs. Use white wine, beer, or just stock or water. If you're a couscous maker, that is the usual Moroccan accompaniment, but rice or boiled potatoes are nice as well.

My friend Mike, a fellow cook and a surfer and painter who lives mostly in El Salvador, suggested we try to come up with a version of that country's **gallo en chicha**. Authentic gallo en chicha is a rooster cooked in a beverage traditionally made by women, who chew corn kernels, spit them out, and then ferment the resulting mash via enzymes from their saliva. We substituted beer for the chew-brew and hen for the rooster, and added sweet red chilies, raisins, and little doses of clove, cinnamon, and brown sugar. Sprinkle toasted pine nuts and chopped fresh or crushed dried oregano on the finished dish and serve with rice or potatoes boiled and then simmered in with the chicken for 5 minutes.

When my son Milo was six, he really liked to draw birds. He'd lie on the floor for hours, wedged-open Peterson Guide under an elbow, rendering determined avian portraits, intent, it seemed, on inscrib-ing pictorial notes for some later use. He also made several series of Sculpey sculptures, mainly of the raptor and woodpecker families, and one winter, during a trip to New York City, he cataloged in his spiral notebook the entire feathered contents of a huge cabinet-lined corridor in the Natural History Museum.

Was there, I wondered years later as I shook the excess flour off of a handful of chicken wings I was frying in batches, a connection between Milo's early intense interest in birds and his current equally intense en-thusiasm for eating a lot of chicken wings? I frankly hoped not—better that artists not eat their models—though I was glad he liked wings; I like them, too. But deep-fried and coated in butter and Tabasco was more happy hour than dinner hour. I needed to find some other ways to cook them because, in addition to being popular with Milo and the other boys, here's what's so good about wings:

1. They're pretty inexpensive.

2. Half of them are like tasty little two-bite drumsticks.

3. The other half are, in their own double-jointed way, just as delicious.

4. A happy crisp-tasty-skin to tender-flavorful-meat ratio is how they fly so high.

Often we do just coat wings with lots of ground coriander and fennel seeds and a pinch of paprika or cayenne and roast them in a hot oven for a nice snack. But when wings are what's for dinner, we braise them just like legs.

Sometimes when we can't find our gumption, we use this even easier, less messy method that is only slightly less good while still being really, really good. To make up for it, we gave this recipe a great name: **Fricken Wings Chicassee**. Season the wings with salt and pepper, spread them in a single layer in a casserole dish, and roast them in a 450°F oven until browned, about 15 minutes. Meanwhile, cook some chopped onions in butter or oil till softened. Add 2 tablespoons flour and cook, stirring, for a minute or two over low heat. Add the garlic and any of the herbs or spices suggested in the braises on page 214–15, cook for 30 seconds, and then stir in wine or beer, water or stock. Bring to a boil over high heat and combine with the wings either by pouring the onion mixture over them in the casserole or fitting them into the skillet. Put the whole thing back in the oven and cook until very tender, about 20 minutes or so. Great with rice to handle the sauce, a salad to keep it fresh, and a sprinkle of gremolata (page 246) or Salsa Verde (page 244) for extra credit.

BRAISED DUCK LEGS

Duck legs require a little more salt and a long, slow cooking to render their generous share of fat, tenderize the rich meat, and take the skin to that mahogany crispness that has earned them their well-deserved reputation for deliciousness. The only real demand of this recipe is time; in fact, it's so easy, and became such a standard in our house, that the kids started complaining, "Duck legs again?" We should all be so abused.

5 duck legs (drumstick and thigh together)	2 celery stalks, roughly chopped
	2 garlic cloves, cut in half
A sprinkle more than 1½ teaspoons salt	3 thyme sprigs
	3 parsley sprigs
Freshly ground black pepper	1 bay leaf
4 tablespoons light olive oil or vegetable oil	¾ cup wine or beer
1 yellow onion, roughly chopped	3 cups chicken stock (page 206) or water
1 large carrot, roughly chopped	

Season the duck legs with salt and pepper and leave at room temperature for 30 minutes or up to a few hours while you prepare the braising ingredients. Or refrigerate them overnight for cooking the next day.

Preheat the oven to 450°F.

Heat a skillet over high and add the oil, then the onion, carrot, and celery. Stir until it gets going, lower the heat to medium, and cook, stirring occasionally, until soft and lightly browned, 15 to 20 minutes. Add the garlic, thyme, parsley, bay leaf, and wine and bring to a simmer. Slip the duck legs in, skin side down, and nestle them into the skillet. Add the stock so that the liquid nearly covers them. Bring back to a simmer, cover the skillet with foil or a lid, and put in the oven for 5 minutes, and then lower the heat to 325°F. (If cooking more legs than will fit in a skillet, braise them in a casserole or baking dish instead.) Cook for 20 minutes and then take the skillet out of the oven, uncover, and turn the duck legs over so that the skin side is up (try to handle the legs by the drumstick end so that you don't tear up the skin). Into a bowl set under a sieve, tip off enough of the liquid so that all the skin is above the tide line but there's still some juice underneath (reserve the

liquid in the bowl; a small, deep-sided one will make the degreasing process easier later). You may have to shift things around a bit so that all the skin is exposed and can get browned and crispy. Continue cooking until very tender and well browned, 45 minutes to 1 hour.

To check for doneness, grab the drumstick bone with tongs and the end of the thighbone with your other hand protected by a kitchen towel. Bend the ends toward each other, and if it feels like you could easily make them touch, it's done. If the joint still feels springy, cook the legs more. If the liquid has evaporated and only fat remains with the vegetables, add back some of the reserved liquid. If the skin is getting very dark and the meat does not yet seem tender, re-cover the skillet before cooking a little longer. When the legs are done, set them aside and strain the remaining contents of the skillet into the bowl with the reserved liquid. Discard the vegetables and herbs (or push them through the sieve with the back of a spoon to thicken and sweeten the juice), and set aside for 5 minutes to allow the fat to rise to the top. With a small ladle, skim off the collected fat and discard (or save for browning boiled potatoes or toasting croutons in). Recombine the braising liquid with the duck, bring back to a simmer, and pop back into the oven for 5 minutes. Eat right away with vegetables or a sturdy green salad and a starch from Chapter 7 to sop the sauce. Fresh sage and rosemary, chopped in restrained amounts and stirred into Salsa Verde (page 244), go great with duck.

Add a couple tablespoons of all-purpose flour in with the garlic and fresh herbs and stir for a few minutes before adding all **red wine** and no stock for **duck-o-van**. As it is with coq au vin, sliced-up bacon is good here, prunes are a sweet surprise, and some sage leaves are not unwelcome. Pick the plumped prunes out of the skillet before straining the vegetable mixture and serve them with the duck. Make Rustic Oily Croutons (page 25) toasted with duck fat instead of the olive oil and sprinkle these decadent nuggets on top.

Use equal parts white wine and sherry, or all **sherry**, and add some **green olives** to the skillet with the duck legs. You can replace the onion with leeks, and a spriglet of rosemary or savory gets along well. If you have some tomatoes, fresh or canned, chop them up and let them join in. Degrease, but don't strain out the leeks and olives—serve them with the duck legs.

Braised duck will happily sit next to **white beans** at the table. In fact, all beans and braises make good tablemates.

Duck legs, and all braised meats, make great **sauce for pasta**. You may want to cook some extra just for that. Pull the meat off the bones and shred it with your hands or chop with a knife. Cook some diced onion, carrot, and celery until very soft, lightly caramelized, and starting to melt together, about 30 minutes. Add some chopped tomato if you like and cook 10 minutes more before adding the duck and the braising liquid. Simmer to bring it all together and toss in your cooked pasta and some chopped parsley if you have it. A tablespoon or two of butter can help if it seems like it needs a little smoothing and cling. Duck, chicken, and pork braises made into ragù sauce like this also really satisfy when spooned over soft Polenta (page 158) or Thick Soft Toast (page 23). A little salad or some garlicky cooked greens and it's dinnertime.

TWICE-COOKED PORK

We started calling this Ping-Pong Pork after a Fourth of July party that grew and grew until we had to move it outside and eat in the backyard, seating our friends around the Ping-Pong table. (We took down the net to prevent side taking and squabbles. Didn't work.) Ping-Pong Pork is really a variation on Mexican carnitas, in which the meat is not so much braised as it is gently boiled. It can be completely cooked ahead and in fact is quite a bit better if seasoned one day, boiled the next, and grilled on the third. Three-day pork, now that sounds impressive—and hard—but it's really very easy. This is the perfect-for-a-party pork that allowed me time to drink a beer and lose a couple of games of Ping-Pong to Milo at what turned out to be the dinner table, before quickly grilling up crispy, tender slabs of pork shoulder.

As a bonus, this recipe yields flavorful (if a little salty) pork stock that can be used later for soup making.

4 pounds pork shoulder, seasoned for an hour at room temperature or overnight in the refrigerator	1 celery stalk
	1 bay leaf
2 teaspoons salt	3 parsley sprigs
Freshly ground black pepper	3 thyme sprigs
1 yellow onion, halved	1 bottle of beer or a glass of white or red wine
1 large carrot	

Put all the ingredients into a big pot and add enough water to cover the pork by 3 inches (about 2 quarts). Bring to a boil over high heat, lower to a simmer, and skim off any foam that rises to the top. Simmer until the meat is quite tender, about 3 hours. Test for doneness by inserting a slender-bladed knife into the meat. It should pull out easily with very little grab. Carefully remove the pork to a large bowl that's higher than the top of the meat. Let the cooking liquid cool a little, then ladle off the impressive layer of fat that a pork shoulder produces. Strain enough of the cooking liquid over the pork to cover it. Refrigerate, uncovered, until completely cooled.

Take the meat out of the broth an hour before you're ready to grill it and slice it 1½ inches thick. When your grill is good and hot (see Chapter 11 for more on grilling), rub a few drops of oil onto the slices and grill them until well browned and crispy on both sides. Bring a little of the cooking liquid to a simmer and pour onto the platter with the pork (but not over the slices or they will lose some crispness) for extra juiciness.

Also served on the table-tennis court that year were pickled jalapeños and carrots (page 176), white beans with rosemary and sage (page 50), coleslaw (page 90), and sweet corn polenta (page 161). We rallied a bowl of Pesto (page 136) back and forth to spoon over our pork and beans. Your serve.

If grilling is not part of your plan, brown the pork slices instead in a hot skillet or under the broiler. Or don't brown it at all, and simmer some chunks of carrot and potatoes in the strained liquid. Add cubes of the pork and some peas, spinach, slim wedges of turnips, or segments of green beans when the carrot and potatoes are nearly done. Cook until all the vegetables are tender and serve in a **bowl with plenty of broth** and Salsa Verde (page 244) or gremolata (page 246) sprinkled over.

Add a couple of tablespoons each cumin and coriander seeds and a

mild, dried red chili or two to the cooking liquid. Add cilantro sprigs and a crumble of dried oregano to the herb department. Skip the whole grilling business if you want, and make **carnitas**. Set aside most of the cooking liquid when the pork is done, but leave in most of the fat. Keep cooking the pork in the pot and it will begin to sizzle and sputter. Stir and let it go, getting brown and fried and falling apart deliciously. Tortillas, some tomato salsa, chopped cilantro, or shredded cabbage with a squeeze of lime and Fourth of July becomes Cinco de Mayo!

Leave out the beer and wine and substitute apple cider vinegar for up to half the water and you're making the northern Indian specialty **vindaloo**. Using more vinegar sticks a tangy spike in the fatty pork and raises it in glory; less gives it a softer piquant-poke. Add whole spices to the mix: cloves and cinnamon in restrained amounts; cumin, paprika or sweet red dried chili, turmeric, roughly chopped ginger and garlic in un-restrained amounts; crushed red pepper flakes or cayenne; and a couple spoonfuls of brown sugar. Serve with rice or boiled potatoes and cooked greens or a green salad. Boiled cauliflower tastes nice with Indian flavors, and a spoonful of plain yogurt can cool things down if you got carried away with the cayenne.

11

Grilling is both primal cooking and next-level cooking. It starts with the visceral appeal of a smoky outdoor fire and the smell of sizzling meat and ripens to a deeper, devil's-in-the-details complexity that has kept me reinventing my technique since my first weenie roast. I grill at home all the time and have gone on from sharpening green sticks for hot dogs to cursing flare-ups in Weber kettles, coaxing coals in tiny hibachis, and coveting pricy Tuscan grills before setting out some years ago to build my own, just the way I wanted it. A task that is starting to feel, not uncomfortably, like a life's work, and not least because the way I want it keeps changing. My current version involves a sturdy grate set over an old concrete sink filled nearly to the top with broken bricks. Quirky, not practical, and probably irreproducible, but it meets many of my ideals for good grilling:

• The cooking grate is thick, unenameled cast iron that gets very hot and stays that way. Many grill grates are made of stainless steel wire, which is kind of like grilling on an oven rack—it works okay, but fragile foods like fish will stick. Great meals can be grilled on a steel grate, but as with skillets, cast iron really cooks.

• The grate is large, allowing for maneuvering of things. To be able to flee inevitable flare-ups, you have to be able to move the food to another, cooler part of the grill and to move it back again once things have extinguished a bit. Good grilling means cooking over hot coals, not actual flaming fire. Save that for sitting around, lighting marshmallow torches, or boiling water in your camp kettle.

• The distance between the cooking grate and the coal bed is adjustable. When the fire is so hot that the chicken is burning long before cooking through, you need to be able to adjust the heat, and for grilling, that means raising the grate. Or lowering it, when the coals are cooling, the sun is dipping, and kids and other hungry dogs are circling for their supper.

Having established my preference for an old-sink-full-of-bricks-in-the-backyard setup, I can say that I have happily grilled elsewhere with great success. Webers are good for closed-lid cooking of large roasts, whole chickens, or even turkeys and, when lined with foil, the baking of respectable, if smoky, pizzas. A friend introduced me to an accidental Weber technique that solves the distance-from-heat-to-grate problem nicely. She always closes the top vents and covers the kettle to smother the coals when done cooking and, counter to instructions and intuition, never empties the ashes. Born more of inattention than innovation, her method, over time, raises the height of the heat source. Tightly covering after grilling means the unburned charcoal is extinguished and able to reignite next time, saving fuel and giving the additional benefit of a broader, more consistent fire to cook over. To try it with your Weber, do nothing, and the longer you do, the better it gets—up to a point. Eventually you have to shovel some of those ashes out.

Cheap, sometimes too cheap, a little hibachi grill does a surprisingly good job. The grates, though tiny, are cast iron and height-adjustable (I will warn that the wooden handles tend to catch fire and burn down to the metal, at which point please use pliers). If you're just grilling a few chicken breasts or sausages, as we often are, and especially if you have limited space, I recommend the hibachi.

If you have plenty of room and a yard that won't turn into a brush fire, the Tuscan grill is wonderful. With its much bigger heavy cast-iron grate and adjustability, the Tuscan grill is like a giant hibachi without the base—the fire goes right on the ground and the grate is cantilevered over it. Simple, clever, and effective, but you can't use it on a wooden deck or nice green lawn without getting in trouble.

Whenever possible, I grill over mesquite charcoal, the kind that comes in an impossible-to-open bag and is simply charcoaled chunks of wood—the flavor it gives is more natural than that of briquettes, and it burns hotter and for longer. After giving up on the pull tab and just cutting the damn bag open, we fill a chimney-type fire starter primed with exactly three pages of newspaper, individually and lightly crumpled, put the readied chimney on top

of the grate for better airflow, and set the paper alight. At first the kids just came in for the glory part: striking the match and putting it to paper. Now if I ask one of them to start the fire, they can do the whole thing themselves, helpful little devils.

Though I'm sure my devils would love the spectacle, I don't use lighter fluid—its petroleum stink lingers too long. For similar reasons, only when there's no alternative do I grill on a gas-fueled rig—it's convenient, sure, but the food doesn't taste nearly as good, and you don't really get to light anything on fire, an undeniable grill thrill.

Once the coals are ready and the grill grates are hot, they need to be well cleaned. I use a wire brush for this, but recently my wire brush burned up in all the fun and I have taken to using a brick, or part of one, and that works fine, too. Scrub the grates till all the burned gunk is off, pause, sip beer, and then wipe them down with paper towels or wads of newspaper till they come up clean. A quick swipe with an oiled paper is a good finish. The notion of not cleaning the grill because all that burned stuff gives good grilled flavor is bunk. Clean the grill well and taste tonight's fish, steak, or eggplant, not last weekend's.

Vegetables, meats, poultry, and fish should all be at room temperature, seasoned with salt and pepper, and lightly coated with oil before hitting the hot grill.

You want coals at their hottest for grilling vegetables, fish, and leaner cuts of meat. Chicken breasts, pork tenderloin, steaks, beef, or lamb roasts that have been trimmed of fat will get nice

and browned on a hot grill by the time they are cooked to your liking. The rarer you want the meat, the hotter the grill should be. For fatter or fattier cuts such as chicken legs, nicely marbled chops, or roasts with some fat on them, you need to grill more slowly and be ready to move the food away from any flame-ups. The black soot that shows up immediately when flame hits food, unlike good dark grill marks, doesn't taste good. Avoid it by keeping the grill cooler or moving to safer ground, which sometimes means taking everything completely off the grill and letting the fire burn down a bit. If (when) flare-ups do happen, wipe the soot off with a paper towel or napkin.

Fragile foods such as fish can stick to the grill and break up when you try to turn them. To avoid this, many otherwise sensible people wrap fish in aluminum foil before "grilling" it. The fish doesn't stick, but neither is it grilled. Cod, sole, halibut, and other flaky fish are simply better cooked an-

other way. Sturdier fish such as mackerel, salmon, and tuna, on the other fin, are great grilled. They, and indeed all grilla-bles, will go on and come off the grate better if it's clean and hot, and the food is left in place as long as possible to develop a caramelized crust that will re-lease and allow for a spatula to slip under. (Giving cover to un-sightly patches left by inevitable grill-stick is yet another of salsa verde's virtues. Be smart: Make a batch before lighting the grill).

The best way to determine doneness is to make a little cut

and peek. If there's a side that looks better and that you'll want facing up, cut into the other side so it can be hidden. Cut-and-peek works for things like steaks, chops, fish, and chicken and at night requires a flashlight. If you're grilling a thicker roast, use a meat thermometer or do what I do and insert a slender-bladed knife into the middle of the meat. Count to five, pull it out, and feel it on the back of your hand or lower lip. Cool: not done. Warm: done. Hot: too done. Let roasts sit for 10 minutes in a warm place before slicing.

Platters, tongs, and spatulas that touch raw meats should be cleaned or switched out before touching cooked final results. I unscientifically sterilize tongs by thrusting them through the grate to be licked clean by purifying flames, though soap and hot water are also effective, if less poetic. You'll need a clean, warm platter for the grilled food to land on, and you may want to warm the oven while you're at it in case you need a few minutes to keep things from cooling down while you set the table or finish a side dish.

When I'm in the kitchen, I'm a chef, but when I'm at the grill, I become something else. For many men, grilling is the only cooking they ever really do, and I feel that kinship with my gender—professional giving way to happy amateur as I step into the fraternal smoke. If I differ from my fellow grillmen, it's in the frequency with which I'll fire up the coals, though I'm motivated grillward not only by manly mandate: I also appreciate the savings in greasy-pan-cleanup that a grilled meal offers the whole family. Of course, I can also wax savory and am a sucker for . . . the way a **chicken leg**, **breast**, or **wing** can be transformed by a dense speckling of black and red pepper and a confident char . . . the way the decadence of pork fat—crisped and rendered sweet—on a **chop** or **a slice of shoulder** (page 222) can be set off by a bowl of spicy pickled jalapeño peppers (page 176) . . . **fish**, **shrimp**, or **squid** seared over red-hot embers, landed on a plate of beans, and dolloped with fragrant aïoli (page 249) . . . **lamb leg** roasts or **beef steaks**, grilled hard and sliced thin, on the arm of a crisp, cool shaved vegetable salad (page 82) and wearing a laurel of anchovy Salsa Verde (page 244) . . . platters of grilled **tomatoes, eggplant, and zucchini** flank to flank with platters of grilled **spiced meatballs** (page 122) and passed with bowls of raita (page 94) . . . **onions and scallions**, and never more so than when they are grilled and glistening with oil . . . **boiled asparagus or fennel** wedges (page 171) that need just a short stay above the hot coals and a little extra sprinkle of salt . . . crusty **Polenta** (page 158) . . . and the elegant simplicity of a thick slice of good **bread**, soft and crunchy, smoke countered by a swipe of garlic and a dose of olive oil.

There's another way to make "grilled" steak that doesn't require a grill. It's called **pan-fried steak** and it does require a good heavy skillet, preferably cast iron. Heat the skillet as if it were a grill—that is, get it very hot, smoking even. Instead of adding oil to the skillet, where it would surely burn or even flash into flames, coat the room-temperature

seasoned meat with oil and then carefully lay it in the skillet. Leave it in place to get well browned before turning. If you're cooking an especially thick payday sort of steak, you may want to finish the cooking in the oven. Be sure the oven is hot at 450°F and that the handle of your skillet is not going to melt, and when the first side is nicely browned, turn the steak over, put the whole thing in the oven, and cook to your desired doneness (by the way, should I ever be crowned king, that's how I will insist on being addressed: Your Desired Doneness). Steaks, and all meats, benefit from resting for 5 minutes before serving. When flush and feeling luxurious, I like rib-eye, New York, or tenderloin steaks. Skirt steak is decadent with fat and flavor and should rest a couple of extra minutes before being sliced across the grain. **Pork chops** and **chicken breasts** can be cooked the same way and all are very good with Salsa Verde (page 244) of any sort, the steak with anchovies especially.

12

I once worked alongside a cook whose real job was as a Boston firefighter. Days he rode the hook and ladder, dousing flames. Nights we stoked the wood-fired rotisserie together and took orders for tea-soaked chickens and smoky grilled pork chops. While we sweated out our shifts, he told me about his life as the best cook in the firehouse. The firemen were big on nicknames: a spark was what they called an arsonist; Sauce was what they called my coworker. I was always jealous of that name— they called him Sauce because he made such good food. Sometimes that's what dinner, not to mention life, needs: a little sauce.

In French cooking, there are the five mother sauces, and my friend Sauce had many more, I'm sure, but for me, it's mostly these three: Salsa Verde, Mayonnaise, and Béchamel. The sauce sisters—a trio so fertile that their little sauce-lets are scattered across tables globally: salsas verde are as numerous as there are varieties of green herbs; mayonnaise, simply oil bound with egg, two ingredients found the world round; béchamel, so powerful and versatile, can even transcend sauce-hood itself.

Well learned and wisely used, these three will bring sustenance, satisfaction, and companionship into your life.

BÉCHAMEL

Béchamel, or white sauce, is familiar to anyone who has ever eaten macaroni and cheese. It's simply milk that is thickened with roux, which is simply flour cooked in butter. A sauce of few, easily found ingredients and not hard to make, béchamel nevertheless requires attention and scorches easily if ignored, even for a minute. Cooking on the edge of total failure like this is exciting, yes, but settle down before you start this recipe: you can't safely walk away from your post for the first 15 minutes, so get your head right, stay hydrated, take no calls.

4 tablespoons (½ stick) butter	2 cups whole milk
3 tablespoons all-purpose flour	Salt

Melt the butter over very low heat in a small saucepan. Add the flour and stir with a whisk for 3 minutes. Raise the heat to medium and add a little of the milk, about ¼ cup, whisking constantly. Ordinarily, adding liquid has a thinning effect, but with béchamel, the milk will do the opposite, making it thicken considerably and get chunky and dry looking. Whisk until the milk is completely mixed in and then add another dose of milk. Again, whisk until all the same consistency. Repeat, whisking all the while, always waiting to add more milk until the last addition is fully incorporated. Raise the heat to medium halfway through the milk additions. When the sauce has the thickness of heavy cream, stir in all the remaining milk and raise the heat to medium-high. It will now be rather thin but will thicken up again when it comes to a boil. Switch from the whisk to a wooden spoon or a rubber spatula that can take the heat and continue stirring, being sure to cover every spot of the bottom of the pan to prevent scorching. Stir and stir until the béchamel just begins to simmer. You may have to pause, but briefly, in your diligent stirrage to be able to detect the subtle turbidity of a murmuring white sauce. Once simmering is confirmed, turn the heat to the lowest setting, stir a minute more, and cover incompletely. Continue to cook, stirring occasionally, for 10 minutes more. Season lightly with salt and the sauce is ready for your plan.

Macaroni and cheese: Stir grated cheese into the béchamel. Gruyère is classically good, cheddar too, and this is a natural place to use up the various ends of cheeses that may be around. Let the béchamel cool slightly before adding the cheese or it can break and look curdled (if it does, fix it like magic in a blender). Cook short pasta like elbows or penne and stir them with the cheese sauce. Serve just like that or turn out into a baking dish, top with oily crumbs (Crumb 2, page 26) or a little more grated cheese, and bake till bubbly and brown, 5 to 10 minutes in a 400°F oven.

Stir some Parmesan into the béchamel and layer it with sheets of cooked pasta, mozzarella or ricotta cheese, and tomato sauce and/or Sautéed Greens (page 190) or mushrooms, starting and ending with pasta layers. Cover with foil and bake the resulting **lasagna** in a 375°F oven until hot in the center (poke a knife in to check) and bubbling around the edges. Uncover, turn up the heat to 450°F, and bake for another 5 to 10 minutes to brown the top. Let cool for 5 minutes before cutting and serving.

Cooked vegetables (Chapter 8), dressed with béchamel and then baked, become a **vegetable gratin**. Add grated Parmesan, Gruyère, or cheddar cheese to the béchamel, if you like, and stir with the vegetables in a mixing bowl. Chopped fresh herbs can be mixed in as well. Spread in a shallow baking dish and spoon over a little more of the béchamel. Bake in a hot oven until bubbling and browned. Cooking times will vary with the size of the vegetables and the depth of the dish. Sprinkle the top with more cheese and/or oily toasted bread crumbs (Crumb 2, page 26) for the final few minutes of baking. Try making a gratin with boiled vegetables like cauliflower or broccoli florets, thick coins of leeks, slices of celery, wedged fennel, or asparagus spears cut in lengths . . . sautéed spinach or

other greens (page 190) with some sautéed onion and garlic . . . wedges
of roasted onion and sautéed mushrooms with a little chopped thyme . . .
and, in the spirit of furthering the search for more delicious ways to cook
zucchini, I offer a very simple gratin made not with béchamel but with
cream: Thinly slice zucchini and toss with salt, chopped garlic, grated
Parmesan, and chopped fresh herbs such as thyme or sage, basil or parsley. Spread flat in a greased baking dish and pour on enough cream to
nearly, but not quite, cover the slices. Too much cream and the gratin will
be awash once the zucchini begins to cook and contribute its considerable
holdings of water. Bake, uncovered, in a 400°F oven until browned, bubbling, and fragrant, about 30 minutes. With a spatula, push down on the

gratin a couple of times during the first part of baking, then stop pushing and sprinkle a little more cheese on near the end.

Add eggs and a little more technique and vegetable gratin becomes the Italian dish **sformato**, a savory baked pudding, like soufflé for the fallen. Start with 2 pounds of vegetables such as cauliflower, celery, or fennel. Boil in salted water until tender, drain, and puree in a blender, food processor, or food mill, adding a little milk if needed to get it going. Make béchamel with 2 tablespoons butter, 1½ tablespoons flour, and 1 cup milk. While the béchamel is cooking, generously butter a baking dish and heat the oven to 400°F. Stir the béchamel into the vegetable puree and mix in 2 beaten eggs and ½ cup grated cheese (Parmesan, fresh chèvre, cheddar, Gruyère). Pour into the prepared dish and bake until just set in the middle, about 30 minutes. Serve immediately, or you can bake the sformato ahead, let cool, and then reheat in a hot oven for 10 minutes.

Béchamel transcends itself when fried into crispy little **croquettas** like they serve in tapas bars. Make béchamel with 5 tablespoons butter, ½ cup all-purpose flour, and 1¼ cups whole milk. The sauce will be very thick. Keep stirring over medium heat until it begins to pull away from the sides and bottom of the pan, about 10 minutes. Stir in salt and some or all of the following: ¼ cup grated cheese (cheddar, Parmesan, Pecorino, manchego), diced ham, boiled peas, or tiny sliced green beans. Spread this fritter mixture on a plate and refrigerate until solid, at least an hour. Beat an egg in a small bowl and put dry bread crumbs (Crumb 1, page 26) in another. With moistened hands, make little balls or cylinders with the fritter mixture. In batches, coat them with the egg, drip off the excess, and then roll them in the bread crumbs to coat completely. Set the fritters on a plate lightly sprinkled with bread crumbs and refrigerate for at least 30 minutes to set the breading. You can refrigerate for up to a day. Shallow- or deep-fry the fritters in batches (see fried vegetables, page 177, for more on frying). Sprinkle with salt and eat hot, standing up, with cold drinks.

Swing herb bunches by their stems to dry—and to celebrate!

SALSA VERDE

Salsa verde is a green herb sauce with an olive oil base. It is, hands down, the sauce I make most often. I'll spoon it over grilled (Chapter 11) or braised (Chapter 10) meats or boiled vegetables (page 171), and often we'll pass a bowl of salsa verde around the table because there are really very few things in this book that wouldn't like to be seen with some sort of salsa verde. There are many variations; the best known is basil pesto; the most basic, parsley and garlic. The olive oil for salsa verde can be your best spicy and fruity bottle, but lightly flavored basic oil works well also.

Some kids have to wash the car; my kids wash the parsley, and here's how: fill a big bowl with cold water and dip the whole bunch of parsley in, swishing it around like you mean it. Lift it, give it a preliminary shake, and then drip as little as possible on the floor as you walk quickly outside. Swing the bunch by the stems, flick it like a whip, spritz the sidewalk, the yard, the dog, the world. Bunches of basil, cilantro, or mint can be taken on the same ride. Set the bunch on a towel to dry off for 5 minutes—herbs chop up nicer and fluffier and don't clump up when they are not wet. To chop a quantity of parsley effectively, pick the leaves from the stems and gather them together into a ball, holding them down on the cutting board as if they were trying to run away. Slice the parsley bundle thinly, as if it were a single vegetable. As you slice, the ball will come apart, but just bunch it back together as best you can, keep slicing, and you'll have a nice head start on the chopping that remains. Hold the tip of the knife on the cutting board and use a paper cutter–like motion to chop away at your pile. Go over it a couple of times and then slide the knife under, like a spatula, and flip it over. Continue chopping and flipping until the parsley is the consistency you like.

½ cup finely chopped parsley	½ cup olive oil
½ garlic clove, pounded	Salt

Stir all the ingredients together in a small bowl. If you're pounding the garlic in a mortar, pound some, or all, of the parsley, too, for a smoother-textured salsa. Good on everything.

By my lights, only parsley, **basil, cilantro,** and **chervil** are able to go solo in salsa verde, but all the other herbs are brilliant in ensemble numbers: **rosemary, sage, and savory** should be chopped finely in small amounts and mashed up with the garlic and salt. These three are very strong, especially raw, and too much can taste medicinal. **Thyme** is almost as rough and tough—the kid brother with the little leaves—and all four are good in any combinations with lots of parsley. **Tarragon, oregano, marjoram, and mint** all can be chopped, more or less finely, and stirred into the parsley and oil. Tarragon can get very licorice-like if overused, so go slow with just a few finely chopped leaves at first, and maybe skip the garlic. Loosen up with the oregano and marjoram, and go wild with the mint, mixing in up to equal parts with the parsley.

Adding a chopped **hard-boiled egg** to salsa verde for the first time is a little epiphany, one of those moments when you can feel it all coming together with an almost audible crack. Be ready for it.

A dose of mashed or chopped **anchovies** added to the herbs makes a salsa that's so good on tomatoes, Hard-Boiled Eggs (page 30), and especially on grilled and sliced lamb or beef.

Capers give a nice complexity and will work with all the herbs mentioned. Their floral nature mixes especially well with chervil or tarragon. Salsa verde made with, in descending amounts, chopped parsley and hard-boiled egg, chervil, capers, and tarragon is very nice on chicken, boiled vegetables, hot or cold, and fish such as salmon, mackerel, and sole.

Red onion, shallot, or **scallion** can be dressed separately in a little lemon juice or red wine vinegar and stirred into the salsa just before serving (if added too early, the lemon/vinegar will make the herbs lose their bright green color . . . salsa brutta).

Diced **celery hearts,** chopped **pickles** of all sorts, green or black **olives,** and **citrus zests** all make good additions to green salsa.

Gremolata is a salsa verde without the oil: just finely chop parsley, garlic, and lemon zest together and sprinkle on most things, especially braises and fried foods.

MAYONNAISE

When I first learned to make mayonnaise and discovered that it was just oil magically held together (emulsified, if science is your magic) with egg yolk, I realized why I liked it so much: a little coating of oil makes things taste better. That's why we all cook with oil, dress salads with it, dip our bread into it. And why we spread mustardy mayonnaise on our sandwich, eat fried fish with tartar sauce, and stir aïoli into soup. If you recoil at the thought of mayonnaise, the very word even, then perhaps, like me, you had a traumatic encounter with a jarred version at a young age. Now I love it—maybe it's time to update *your* outlook and make a batch.

1 egg yolk

1 teaspoon Dijon mustard

Salt

1 cup light olive oil (spicy olive oil can make mayonnaise bitter)

1 teaspoon red wine vinegar

1 teaspoon lemon juice

Whisk the egg yolk, mustard, and salt together in a small bowl. The size matters here: the oil whisks into the egg yolk more readily in a snug vessel. It doesn't make sense, but somehow a mortar and pestle also works. Add the oil, drop by drop at first, stirring all the while. Drip slowly and stir quickly until the yolk begins to hold the oil and thicken, about a quarter of the way through. Now you can pour the oil a little quicker, in a stream, but you cannot stop stirring. Find a friend if you're getting tired. Keep going and at about the ½ cup mark, the emulsion tends to get a little too thick, so add a teaspoon of water. Use all the oil, and then stir in the vinegar and lemon. If the mayonnaise looks very shiny and bouncy, add a little more water to smooth it out.

If your mayonnaise breaks and looks curdled and separated, **fix it** by starting a new egg yolk in a new bowl. Get the emulsion started with drops of oil and then start adding your broken mayonnaise little by little. Stir in a spoonful of water if it gets too tight.

For **aïoli**, replace the mustard with a pounded garlic clove (or as many as you're ready for). Stir in the oil mayonnaise-style. Forgive me, France, but I like a little vinegar or lemon in aïoli. A good place to start thinking about all that aïoli can do is le Grand Aïoli: the classic platter of simply cooked fish, sliced summer tomatoes, Hard-Boiled Eggs (page 30), boiled potatoes, and other vegetables such as green beans and fennel in summer, and carrots and beets in winter (page 171)—served with a bowl of aïoli to pass and dip and dollop. Aïoli really feels as if it belongs when stirred into a bowl of warm beans or chickpeas, especially if there are also shrimp, clams, or squid swimming in there.

Finely chop or pound fresh **herbs** in a mortar, add some of the oil to them, and then stir into the mayonnaise. Mayonnaise with parsley, basil, chervil, or chives is great with fish, boiled vegetables, sandwiches, anything fried, Hard-Boiled Eggs (page 30), and roasted beets.

To make **tartar sauce**, finely dice some shallots or slice scallions and set aside dressed with a little lemon juice or vinegar. Chop parsley and chives, chervil, or tarragon, and any combination of capers, cornichons, celery hearts, and Hard-Boiled Eggs (page 30) and stir into the mayonnaise. Add a teaspoon of mustard, a pinch of cayenne, and the shallots or scallions. Mix well. Classic with fried fish (page 179) and damn good on a sandwich.

Milo sometimes likes to skip all of the above, stir some ketchup into jarred mayonnaise, and call it **special sauce**. When he's feeling expansive, he'll shake in some Crystal hot sauce, and if we ever kept pickle relish on hand, he'd surely spoon some in. Chopped quickles (page 175) or Mexican-style pickles (page 176) would work. We smile and tease him for his lack of sophistication as, in spite of ourselves, we dip in.

13

When the moon is full, we like to bake a cake. Birthdays come but once a year and that's too long to wait between cakes, especially when the white-frosted moon shows up monthly for inspiration. For years, we used a recipe that was quite simple for the kids to make, but we finally had to admit it was simply not very good. Still, when we'd dust it with powdered sugar to make it moonier, and drink glasses of milk to ease its dry crumb, we would gaze up at the full-faced model for our creation and eat a slice.

Even if you're not so lunar, you'll at least want to bake a cake when a birthday boy or girl is around, because we all know that there are few times sweeter than when someone bakes you a cake: you blow out the candles when the singing stops, and that first bite of homemade birthday cake is like the first flush of love—flaw becomes endearment; char, charm; crumb, morsel. Birthday cake works this magic because baking a cake from scratch can be a pain and everybody knows it, so the effort is noticed. Though I have found some ways to simplify these recipes, I will probably always struggle with the counting part, the measuring part, the forgetting-it-in-the-oven part. But I bake on, counting on my fingers, staying focused, and using a timer. Baking with a kid, or someone who acts like one, helps me to laugh at the mess while we fight over who gets to lick the spoon.

I loved baking with my mom and then with friends when I was younger, but the creaming-the-butter part of the recipe really burned me up with its near-impossibility. How could they expect you to take a wooden spoon to two cold sticks of butter and a cup of sugar and come up with something "light" and "fluffy"? I thought they were messing with me until the day I learned that baking cakes (and cookies) is so much easier when you take the refrigerated ingredients—butter, eggs, yogurt, milk—out to come to room temperature for an hour or two. Seems like a long time to wait, but if you skip this step and use cold ingredients, the whole thing is much harder, especially creaming the dang butter. So go for a walk or read or clean something. You can even take all but the milk out in the morning, go about your day's business, and bake when you get home in the evening—they'll be fine unrefrigerated.

Since temperatures vary from oven to oven, baking time is not a set thing. The most common culprit when my cakes aren't all I hoped they'd be is overbaking. Waiting until the exact time that a recipe calls for can mean you are too late and that the cake is overcooked. If the recipe says to bake for 30 minutes, start checking at 20—carefully; you don't want to bring your cake crashing down with a jerk of the oven rack at a sensitive moment. Peek in, give the pan a tiny nudge, and look for jigglyness in the center. If the cake wobbles and looks soft and crinkled on top, gently close the door, tiptoe away, and set the timer for a few more minutes. If it's looking set, slide out the rack and touch the top of the cake with your fingers, testing for bounce-back. If your touch leaves a dent that stays, back in with it. If it does spring back, the final test is sticking a toothpick into the center. When it comes out moist but crumb-free, it's cake time! After it cools . . . after it cools.

CHOCOLATE MISTAKE CAKE

Mistakes are like vengeful kitchen gods. They cook side by side with us, ever ready to step in and put a finish to that dish. There's no losing them, so we invite them to the table to teach us what they can. There are moments in the making of this cake that seem like disasters. That they are not is delightful, but when they do show up, we'll be ready, saying, "Hey, Mistakes, sit down. I baked you a cake. Happy birthday!"

8 tablespoons (1 stick) butter	2 teaspoons baking soda
1½ cups boiling water	½ teaspoon salt
4 ounces bittersweet chocolate, chopped up, or bittersweet chocolate chips	2½ cups (lightly packed) brown sugar
	½ cup plain whole-milk yogurt
2 cups all-purpose flour	2 teaspoons pure vanilla extract
½ cup unsweetened cocoa powder	3 eggs

Preheat the oven to 350°F.

Cut the stick of butter into ½-inch-thick slices. Reserve the butter wrapper. Put the butter in a large mixing bowl, add the boiling water, wait a moment, and then add the chocolate and leave aside to melt. Use the butter wrapper to grease the sides and bottom of an 8- or 9-inch cake pan.

In a medium mixing bowl, sift together the flour, cocoa, baking soda, and salt and set aside.

Add the sugar and yogurt to the chocolate-and-butter mixture and stir with a whisk until it no longer looks, as Liam says, "like a distant galaxy." Add the vanilla and the eggs, one at a time, and whisk each time until smooth. Whisk in half the dry ingredients, stir till nearly mixed in, and then add the other half. Stir with the whisk until completely smooth and pour into the prepared pan. Put in the oven and start checking for doneness in 25 minutes (see page 252); the cake should be done at around 35 minutes.

You might also want to offer a dollop of whipped cream, a spoonful of vanilla ice cream or frozen yogurt, or a cold glass of milk to go with that fat slice.

CARROT CAKE

Carrot cake is splendid for several reasons:

- It's kind of healthy seeming with the carrots, walnuts, and raisins.

- No beating butter senseless—in fact, frosting aside, no butter at all.

- It was our wedding cake, and why? Because of all the fluffy, white-wedding, cream cheese frosting It's what draws my kids to it, I'm sure, but they do appreciate as well the moistness of a crumb that stays that way till morning, when it's very good—if a bit sweet—for breakfast.

Oil or butter, for the pan

1¼ cups all-purpose flour

1 teaspoon baking powder

¼ teaspoon salt

½ teaspoon ground cinnamon

⅓ cup granulated sugar

½ cup brown (lightly packed) sugar

½ cup plain whole-milk yogurt

⅓ cup vegetable oil

2 eggs

½ teaspoon pure vanilla extract

½ pound carrots, grated

½ cup walnuts, toasted (page 11) and chopped

¼ cup raisins

Cream Cheese Frosting (recipe follows)

Grease an 8- or 9-inch cake pan with a little oil or butter and preheat the oven to 350°F.

In a medium bowl, sift together the flour, baking powder, salt, and cinnamon. In a large bowl, whisk together the granulated sugar, brown sugar, yogurt, oil, eggs, and vanilla. Add the dry ingredients to the wet, and when completely blended, stir in the carrots, walnuts, and raisins. Pour into the prepared pan, put in the oven, and start checking for doneness in 35 minutes; the cake should be done at around 45 minutes.

Cool for 30 minutes, then run a table knife around the edge of the pan, top with an upside-down plate, and invert the pan so the cake falls onto the plate. Let cool completely and then frost.

Cream Cheese Frosting

4 tablespoons (½ stick) butter, softened at room temperature

4 ounces cream cheese, softened at room temperature

1 cup powdered sugar (or more if you want it very white and sweet)

Zest and juice of ½ lemon

½ teaspoon pure vanilla extract

In a medium mixing bowl, whisk together the butter and cream cheese until they begin to get fluffy. Add the remaining ingredients and whip until smooth. Frost the cake whole, or cut into layers and frost in between if you want. Refrigerate for at least 1 hour before serving.

Anywhere there are home vegetable gardens, there are zucchini and midsummer neighbors leaving huge, strapping "gifts" in unlocked cars and on unprotected porches. If you find one there, or lurking under your own garden's leaves, you can grate ½ pound instead of carrots and make **zucchini bread**. When feeling less vegetal, replace the carrots with 2 or 3 mashed overripe bananas and the raisins with ½ cup semisweet chocolate chips for **banana bread**. Why is it called cake when made with carrots, and bread when made with zucchini or banana? I ask you. Baked in a loaf pan, it's bread. In a cake pan, cake. Same batter. Go figure.

PLUM UPSIDE-DOWN CAKE

As a child, I loved fruit for dessert, provided it was fruit cocktail and it came from a can of sweet syrup. My brother and sister and I would fight over the bright red cherry—was there really just one?—hidden among the slippery sliced pears, peaches, and pineapple. And though cans of heavy syrup don't figure into desserts for us these days, for the longest time fruit was all I'd serve for dessert at home. When they're at their peak, there's truly nothing that can match slices of crisp tart apples, sunny peach chunks, or a cool bowl of berries. I still feel that way, but sometimes when we want something special we make this upside-down cake. It works well with pears, figs, peeled and sliced oranges (or pineapple, of course!) and is especially appreciated in spring when the plums are peaking.

2 sticks butter, at room temperature	¼ teaspoon salt
¾ cup (lightly packed) brown sugar	1 cup granulated sugar
1½ pounds plums, pitted and sliced into thin wedges	3 eggs, at room temperature
1¾ cups all-purpose flour	1 teaspoon pure vanilla extract
2 teaspoons baking powder	¾ cup milk, at room temperature

Cut ½ stick of the butter into slices and place them and the brown sugar in an 8- or 9-inch cake pan. Set the pan over a medium-high burner. Stir from time to time as the butter and sugar melt together and continue until the mixture gets pale and bubbly, swirly when stirred, and smells toasty brown-buttery, about 2 minutes. Set aside to cool.

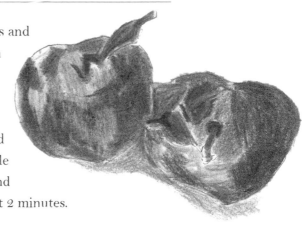

Arrange the plum wedgelets in the cake pan. Liam goes with a simple sun pattern; I attempt a hound's-tooth hatch.

Preheat the oven to 350°F.

In a medium bowl, sift together the flour, baking powder, and salt and set aside. Put the remaining 1½ sticks butter in a large mixing bowl. Beat the heck out of the butter with a wooden spoon until it gets lighter in both color and consistency. Add the sugar and beat some more. Separate the egg yolks from the whites and set the whites aside in a medium bowl. Add the yolks to the butter and sugar, stirring in (you can stop beating now) completely, and then add the vanilla. Add half the dry ingredients and stir until all mixed in. Stir in the milk until completely smooth, then the rest of the dry ingredients just until fully incorporated.

Whisk the egg whites until very fluffy. The whites should look shiny with soft peaks—stop whisking before they look dry and cracky. Gently but thoroughly mix the whipped whites into the batter — all the air that you just whipped in will go out of the whites if you overmix at this point. Pour the batter over the fruit in the pan and smooth the top. Put the cake in the oven and start checking for doneness in 35 minutes; the cake should be done at around 45 minutes.

CAKE-CAKE

"Cake, Dad, can't we just have cake?" Liam asked, channeling Marie Antoinette one birthday. "Not carrot, not upside-down . . . just right-side-up regular cake-cake?"

"Yes, honey, of course we can . . . well, no, not exactly." Flavored discreetly with lemon zest and yogurt, cake-squared is as close to regular as we get. A variation on upside-down cake, without the fruit baked in—Liam prefers it this way—this is the cake we bake at the time of year when the Northern California hills are dry, hot, and scented with ripe blackberries. We tromp out to our berry patches, basket in hand, and while the birthday boy likes to pick and eat, pausing only to slip berries onto his fingertips before eating them off, one by one, pointer to pinky, the rest of us try to save some to take home, toss with a little sugar, and spoon over slices of cake-cake after the cream is whipped and the candles blown out.

1¾ cups all-purpose flour	3 eggs
2 teaspoons baking powder	1 teaspoon pure vanilla extract
¼ teaspoon salt	Zest and juice of ½ lemon
1½ sticks butter	¼ cup milk
1 cup sugar	½ cup plain whole-milk yogurt

Preheat the oven to 350°F.

In a medium mixing bowl, sift together the flour, baking powder, and salt. Put the butter in a large mixing bowl (save the butter wrappers to grease an 8- or 9-inch cake pan, sides and bottom) and beat the heck out of it with a wooden spoon until it gets lighter in both color and consistency. Add the sugar and beat some more. Separate the egg yolks from the whites and set the whites aside in a medium bowl. Add the yolks to the butter and sugar, stirring in (you can stop beating now) completely,

and then add the vanilla and the lemon zest and juice. Add half of the dry ingredients and stir until all mixed in. Stir the milk into the yogurt and then add to the bowl. Mix completely and then add the rest of the dry ingredients, stirring just until fully incorporated.

Whisk the egg whites until very fluffy. The whites should look shiny with soft peaks—stop whisking before they look dry and cracky. Gently but thoroughly mix the whipped whites into the batter—all the air that you just whipped in will go out of the whites if you overmix at this point. Pour the batter into the greased pan and gently smooth the top. Put in the oven and start checking for doneness in 20 minutes (see page 252); the cake should be done at around 30 minutes.

You can also make cake-cake with **whole eggs**, if whipping egg whites seems too daunting today. It makes for a more pound-cake texture and is good—I have discovered, later that night, standing in the light of the open refrigerator door in warm slippers—eaten in cold slivers.

Liam loves **whipped cream**, and why not: it's noisy, tasty, and great with cake-cake, and it looks funny on your brother's face. He likes to help whip, adding only a little granulated sugar and passing the bowl around when his arm gets tired, but what blew his mind was the time someone brought over a *can* of whipped cream. His look of puzzlement soon turned to adoration as he upended the can and the cream frothed forth with a Bronx cheer. He looked up, awestruck, and whispered, "Automatic!"

PAN CAKE

Maybe you forgot his or her birthday, or maybe you didn't forget, maybe you never even knew, but jeez, it's today, really? This cake won't work for a kid's birthday—that calls for more . . . of everything—but if you just got home, dinner isn't even made, and it turns out it is someone special's day, you just have to bust out a cake, and this one is all from the pantry and requires minimal gear and cleanup. Send him out for a pint of ice cream or suggest she use the shower first—this cake can be in the oven before your celebrant gets back. Thirty minutes later and it's out and cooling on the counter. Fair warning: this cake is like that guy who never moves out of his parents' house—born there, no matter how ready it seems, it falls to pieces when you try to get it out. Cut into wedges and lever them out individually, then cover your tracks with vanilla ice cream or plain or chocolate whipped cream (page 267).

1½ cups all-purpose flour

1 cup sugar

⅛ cup unsweetened cocoa

½ teaspoon salt

1 teaspoon baking soda

1 teaspoon finely ground coffee beans (optional)

1 teaspoon pure vanilla extract

1 tablespoon red or white wine vinegar

⅓ cup vegetable oil

Preheat the oven to 350°F.

Put the flour, sugar, cocoa, salt, baking soda, and ground coffee beans (if using) in an ungreased 8- or 9-inch round cake pan and stir with a whisk. Make a crater, pour in the remaining ingredients and 1 cup water, and whisk until all the corners are gotten and the batter is smooth. Put in the oven and start checking for doneness in 20 minutes (see page 252); the cake should be done at around 30 minutes.

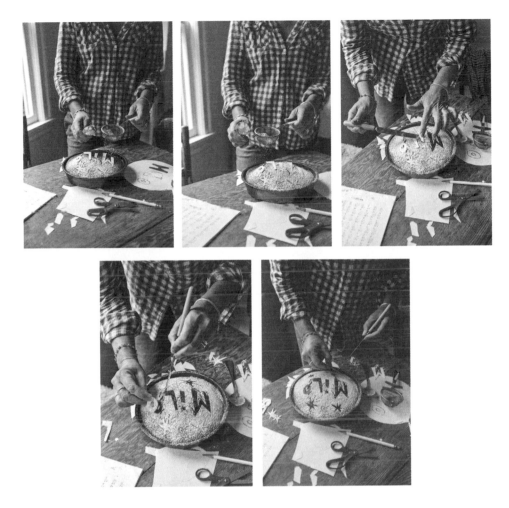

Vanilla ice cream really helps pan cake, and so does **chocolate whipped cream frosting**. Start with 4 ounces of semisweet chocolate, chopped or chips, and 1 pint whipping cream. Put all the chocolate and about ½ cup of the cream in a medium mixing bowl and heat over simmering water until the chocolate has melted. Remove from the heat and whisk in the rest of the cream and 1 or 2 teaspoons sugar. Refrigerate until well chilled and then whip until thick and smooth. Be sure the cake is completely cooled before spreading on. If it's a warm day and you're not eating the cake right away, refrigerate it or the chocolate cream will melt right off.

BLACKBERRY CRISP

For a couple of adolescent years, having finally abandoned his long and robust campaign of lobbying for a video game unit, Milo fixed on a new cause. He would make soda—his own flavors, handcrafted—and market them. He was, I think, not so interested in cashing in—he just wanted the unlimited soda that inevitably would flow and end the parentally imposed drought. We didn't say no, but we weren't particularly helpful in his soft-drink venture, so he was on his own to mash blackberries, wild mint, and tiny sour plums in the bottoms of jars before adding sugar. Bubbly water we begrudgingly supplied. Though Milo loved making these potions (hoping further, perhaps, that one of them might conjure a way out of muggle-hood), the drinks weren't especially good—possibly because we kept the lid on the sugar bowl—and when the soda business went the way of the video console, we started making wild blackberry crisp.

Almost any fruit works in this recipe. In the summer, it's nice to mix nectarines or peaches with the berries. In autumn, pears or apples, maybe mixed with a few raisins or dried cherries, make a delicious crisp. Substitute almonds or hazelnuts for the walnuts if you like. Serve hot, warm, or at room temperature with cream, whipped or not, ice cream, or plain yogurt.

¾ cup walnuts	⅛ teaspoon ground cinnamon (optional)
1¼ cups plus 1½ tablespoons all-purpose flour	½ teaspoon salt
4 tablespoons brown sugar	9 tablespoons cool unsalted butter
4 tablespoons granulated sugar	2 pints blackberries

Preheat the oven to 350°F. Spread the walnuts on a baking sheet and toast until lightly browned, 8 to 10 minutes. When cooled, rub them in a cloth to remove as much of the skins as you can and then chop coarsely.

In a medium mixing bowl, combine the nuts, 1¼ cups flour, brown sugar, 3 tablespoons of the granulated sugar, cinnamon (if using), and salt. Dice the butter as best you can and use your fingers to rub the butter into the flour mixture. You want it to have a moist, crumbly texture that clumps together some and holds its shape when squeezed.

Toss the berries with the remaining 1½ tablespoons flour and the remaining 1 tablespoon of granulated sugar and spread them in a 2-inch deep 7 × 10-inch baking dish (you can also use an 8-inch cast-iron pan). Spread the crumbly topping evenly over the fruit and bake until hot throughout and browned on top, 30 to 40 minutes, depending on the depth of the dish. If the top is getting too dark before the middle is hot, cover with foil and bake a little longer. Let sit for at least 5 minutes before serving.

FROZEN YOGURT

As game a cook as I am, making custard for ice cream has always intimidated me. I think it has to do with the eggs—bless them, can't live without them, but they can be a little scary, always threatening to scramble and scorch. As it so often does, in rides yogurt to my rescue. No cooking is required for frozen yogurt, and though it lacks the richness of ice cream, that's also its charm. We like a scoop of it topped with Orange Ice (page 272) and served with Sesame Cookies (page 275). Get on your bike, Creamsicle! Split, 50/50! Meet the Frozen Open Sesame!

1 cup whole milk	Pinch of salt
½ cup half-and-half	3 cups whole milk yogurt
Scant ½ cup sugar	Zest and juice of ½ lemon
¼ teaspoon pure vanilla extract	

In a large bowl, whisk the milk, half-and-half, sugar, vanilla, and salt together until the sugar is completely dissolved. Stir in the yogurt and lemon zest and juice. Taste and then freeze in your ice-cream machine according to the manufacturer's instructions. Eat soft or transfer to a covered container and let firm up in the freezer for a couple of hours.

Sweetened, mashed-up **berries** can be mixed into, or spooned over, frozen yogurt.

ORANGE ICE

We have an ice-cream machine at home, the kind with the frozen canister and the motorized base, but it doesn't always work right. One day, when our machine started sounding and smelling overheated, we rediscovered this way of making orange ice. We poured the unfrozen juice into a bowl and stuck it in the freezer while old frosty took a rest. By the time we remembered it, the juice was frozen solid. Undeterred, we scraped up fluffy bowls of it, Italian ice–style, and missed only the dry feel of those little wooden shovel-spoons on our lips.

Pour 1 quart of orange juice—the closer to freshly squeezed you can get, the better, but a carton works fine as well—into a mixing bowl and add a scant cup sugar. Stir with a whisk until the sugar is completely dissolved. Taste and add lemon juice and/or zest if it seems to need a little zip. Put the bowl in the freezer and either forget it for 6 hours or stir it once an hour if you're around. Once it's frozen, you can break it up and grind chunks in a food processor until soft and granular, or just scrape the surface with the side of a wide spoon as if you're trying to get the top layer off. The ice will get fluffy and sparkly, light in color and texture. Cover the remainder and keep in the freezer, scraping more when you want more.

Tangerine, clementine, satsuma, and grapefruit juices make wonderful ices a well. For lemon ice, mix 1 cup juice and a little zest with 3 cups water and a cup of sugar.

If your machine isn't broken, you can freeze fruit ices in it as well.

SESAME COOKIES

This cookie is like a combination of the sesame seed candies you might see on the counter at the convenience store and the elegant pain d'amande cookies you might see on the counter at Chez Panisse. Sliced thin and baked crisp, each wafer looks like an underground cross section of the Secret World of Sesame. This recipe makes enough for about 80 cookies, depending on how thinly you slice them, but we usually just bake what we are going to eat that night and save the rest, frozen, to bake another time.

1¼ cups white or golden sesame seeds (or replace ¼ cup with black sesame seeds)

2 cups all-purpose flour

¼ teaspoon baking soda

¼ teaspoon salt

8 tablespoons (1 stick) butter

Scant 1½ cups natural sugar (such as Sugar in the Raw, organic cane sugar, etc.)

⅓ cup boiling water

Heat a skillet to medium and add the sesame seeds. Toast, stirring and tossing until the seeds are lightly browned and fragrant, 2 to 4 minutes. Tip out onto a plate and set aside to cool.

In a medium bowl, sift the flour, baking soda, and salt together. Place the butter and sugar in a large bowl. Let the water cool for 5 seconds, then pour it in and stir. When the butter is all melted, stir in the flour mixture and the sesame seeds. The dough will form a sticky mass.

With damp hands, divide it in 2 sections and pat each half into a slab 4 inches wide and 1 inch thick. Wrap in plastic or waxed paper and freeze flat until you're ready for some cookies (or at least an hour so that they can be thinly sliced). Preheat the oven to 325°F while you cut the frozen dough into slices as thin as you can. Bake them on a cookie sheet until lightly tanned, 8 to 10 minutes. Wait 2 minutes and then use a spatula to transfer the cookies to a platter. They will crisp as they cool in about 10 minutes.

Thank you to:

My wife, Kathleen Henderson, for her generous love and countless lessons in how to see, without which I would surely miss so much beauty in this life.

My son Henderson, for his graceful support, for his keen and critical vision, and for the smile-dimples he, thankfully, hasn't grown out of.

My son Milo, for his astonishing sense of humor, for pulling me along into deeper thinking, and for letting me occasionally win a point, if not a whole game, at the Ping-Pong table.

My son Liam, for his sustaining warmth and affection, for keeping me younger just when I was getting older, and for his uncomplicated love of soup.

Liam, Milo, Henderson, and Kathleen for beautifully illustrating this book (and our home).

My mom and dad; my brother, Dave; and my sister, Katie, for good company around family tables past, present, and future.

Everyone at Chez Panisse, my second home in so many ways, especially my kitchen-mates Nathan Alderson, Carrie Lewis, Mary Jo Thoresen, Jérôme Waag, and Beth Wells. Thanks, Amy Dencler and Gordon Heyder, for making many years, and every Monday, so delicious. Thank you also to Steve Crumley, Renee des Tombe, Noel Diaco, Martin Johnson, Jennifer Sherman, and Jonathan Waters for bringing it forth.

Alice Waters, for her ability to dream of a world fed well, and then cook that world into delicious reality with determination, tenacity, and pleasure.

Michael Pollan, and Alice, for their kind and considerate forewords.

The many former Chez Panisse chefs with whom I had the excellent good fortune to cook with, including Katherine Brandel, Mary Canales, Philip Dedlow, Kelsie Kerr, Christopher Lee, Russell Moore, Jean-Pierre Moullé, Gilbert Pilgrim, Mia Ponce, Leah Puidokas, Lindsey Shere, Peggy Smith, Alan Tangren, and David Tanis.

Tamar Adler, Jenny Bloomfield, Laurel Braitman, Mike Dooley, Charlie Hallowell, Anna Kovel, Mike Marshall, Beth Ann McFaden, Samin Nosrat, and Leah and Mike Wollenburg, for their great friendship and support and for eating the experiments and bringing the wine.

Gordon Drysdale, Lydia Shire and Susan Regis, Stan Frankenthaler and Chris Schlesinger, and Loretta Keller, for hiring me at their wonderful restaurants and showing a young cook how to tie on an apron and step up to the stove.

The Berkeley Public Library, the Montalvo Arts Center, and Cristina Salas-Porras and Lee Hudson at Hudson Ranch for quiet spots to sit down and write.

Cassie Jones, for insightful editing that confirmed my ideas and gracefully improved upon the book I set out to write.

Everyone at William Morrow, including Anna Brower, Andy Dodds, Lynn Grady, Tavia Kowalchuk, Mumtaz Mustafa, Lorie Pagnozzi, Liate Stehlik, Rachel Meyers, and Kara Zauberman.

Sharon Bowers, for her essential guidance and unflagging confidence in me.

Ed Anderson and George Dolese, for making beautiful pictures in the most pleasant sort of way.

Elizabeth David, Marcella Hazan, and Paula Wolfert, for writing the best cookbooks.

Nick Hallowell, for the love of cake.

Steven Newell, for Casa Lacche, where the cooking really started.

Bibo Falk, for housing, hosting, and homing in on what's important.

And to my late, great friend Bobby Buechler, for being the most enthusiastic eater and drinker I have ever known.

Universal Conversion Chart

250 °F = 120 °C

275 °F = 135 °C

300 °F = 150 °C

325 °F = 160 °C

350 °F = 180 °C

375 °F = 190 °C

400 °F = 200 °C

425 °F = 220 °C

450 °F = 230 °C

475 °F = 240 °C

500 °F = 260 °C

MEASUREMENT EQUIVALENTS

Measurements should always be level unless directed otherwise.

⅛ teaspoon = 0.5 mL

¼ teaspoon = 1 mL

½ teaspoon = 2 mL

1 teaspoon = 5 mL

1 tablespoon = 3 teaspoons = ½ fluid ounce = 15 mL

2 tablespoons = ⅛ cup = 1 fluid ounce = 30 mL

4 tablespoons = ¼ cup = 2 fluid ounces = 60 mL

5⅓ tablespoons = ⅓ cup = 3 fluid ounces = 80 mL

8 tablespoons = ½ cup = 4 fluid ounces = 120 mL

10⅔ tablespoons = ⅔ cup = 5 fluid ounces = 160 mL

12 tablespoons = ¾ cup = 6 fluid ounces = 180 mL

16 tablespoons = 1 cup = 8 fluid ounces = 240 mL

INDEX

Note: Page references in *italics* indicate photographs.